An Illustrated History of
Cambodia

An Illustrated History of
Cambodia

Phnom mouy min del mean kla pi
'One mountain cannot have two tigers'
(Khmer proverb)

Philip Coggan

jb

JOHN BEAUFOY PUBLISHING

First published in the United Kingdom in 2018 by John Beaufoy Publishing,
11 Blenheim Court, 316 Woodstock Road, Oxford OX2 7NS, England
www.johnbeaufoy.com

10 9 8 7 6 5 4 3 2 1

ISBN 978-1-912081-97-4

Edited and indexed by Krystyna Mayer
Cartography by William Smuts
Project management by Rosemary Wilkinson

Printed and bound in Malaysia by Times Offset (M) Sdn. Bhd.

Pages 2–3: The Throne Hall in the Royal Palace, Phnom Penh.

Page 5: Ta Prohm has been left as it was found in the late 19th century, enveloped by the jungle.

Page 6–7: Stone carving at Angkor Wat.

CONTENTS

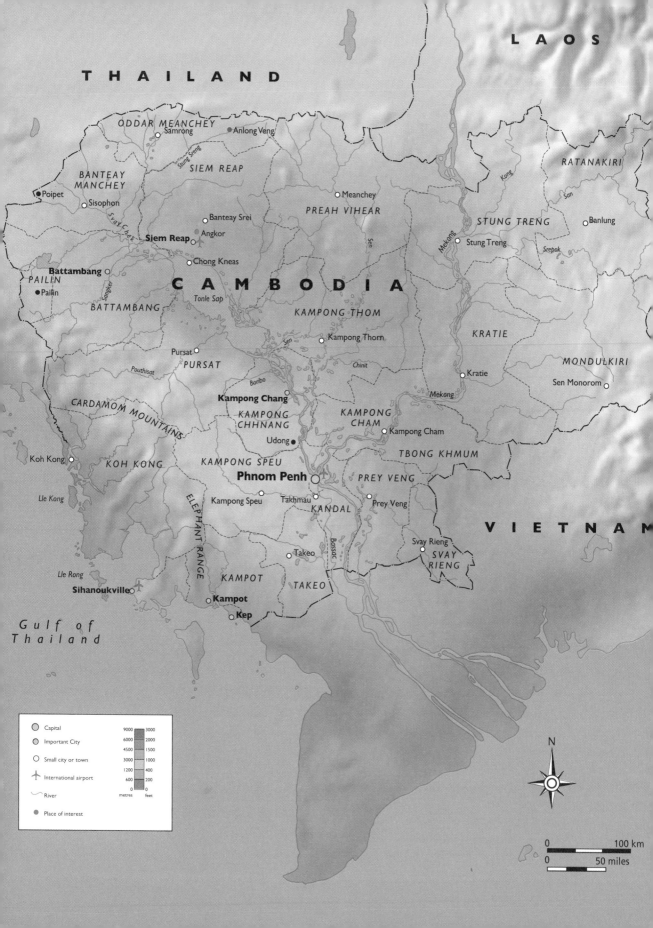

1

DEFINING CAMBODIA
An ancient land

Cambodians call their country Srok Khmer, Land of the Khmers, or on formal occasions Kampuchea, from whence comes French Cambodge and English Cambodia.

In AD 947, about a century and a half after Angkor was founded, a king named Rajendravarman left an inscription tracing his ancestors to the Indian sage Kambu, from whom were descended the Kambuja, the sons of Kambu. There is no Kambu in Indian literature, and the story is no more historical than the attempt of the Anglo-Saxon monk Bede to trace English royalty back to the god Woden. The Indians did, however, know a people called the Kamboja, who lived in the region of modern Kabul in around the 5th century BC, were probably Persian, and did not observe the Hindu caste system or the laws regulating food and marriage. They were, in short, savages, at least in the eyes of good Hindus. They had no connection with Cambodia, but like the Khmer they were distant barbarians on the edges of the Indian world, and the kings of Angkor probably took their name and constructed Kambu from it.

A different and older ancestor legend tells how an Indian prince named Kaundinya sailed to the eastern seas, where he met the naked daughter of the serpent-king and taught her to wear clothes. The princess agreed to marry the prince, and as Cambodia at that time was covered by the sea her father, the naga king, swallowed the water so that their descendants could live in the land of the Khmers.

ANCESTORS

Early in the 20th century, the Indian historian R. C. Majumdar published *Kambuja Desa: An Ancient Indian Colony in Cambodia*, in which he argued that the myths were distant folk memories of a time when Indian colonists brought civilization to the naked aborigines of Southeast Asia. A little later the French scholar George Cœdès, in his *The Indianised States of Southeast*

Asia, correlated Chinese chronicles with Sanskrit inscriptions to identify successive waves of merchants, brahmins and princely adventurers who brought Indian culture to the courts of native chiefs. Like Majumdar, Cœdès believed that the myths and legends had a basis in reality, and he identified two historical Kaundinyas as the founder and Indianizer, respectively, of the Cambodian kingdom.

The idea that Southeast Asians were the passive recipients of Indian civilization at the hands of conquerors and colonists is still found in popular histories, but there is absolutely no evidence to support it, or that there was ever a Kaundinya. Cœdès was reflecting, no doubt unconsciously, the late 19th- and early 20th-century colonial narrative in which European nations brought the blessings of civilization to backward Asians. Majumdar's history was a mirror image, one in which ancient India's status as a source of

MINORITIES

The Vietnamese were estimated in 2014 to number around three quarters of a million. Many are urban, while others live in seasonal fishing villages on the Mekong and around the Tonle Sap. The Chinese are well integrated and almost exclusively urban, and the Muslim Cham live in large farming and fishing villages mostly in the east of the country.

The tribal minorities, called collectively Khmer Loeu, 'highland Khmer', numbered about 100,000 in 1998. They played an important role in Cambodian history and still make up the majority of the population in the north-east, but are coming under pressure from land grabbing and illegal logging.

civilization negated Britain's right to rule his homeland. Both overlooked the fact that mythic ancestors exist to provide glue for national identity, not to preserve a memory of real events.

BOUNDARIES

The Constitution states the motto of Cambodia as 'Nation, Religion, King'. By nation it means all Cambodians, including the non-Khmer minorities, but the Khmer make up well over 90 per cent of Cambodia's population and have a very keen sense of their identity. The French called this 'Khmeritude', Khmer-ness, meaning an attachment to the sacred land of the Khmer ('Srok Khmer'), plus a consciousness of shared language, history and culture. These set the boundaries of ethnic identity.

The Khmer have lived in the valley of the lower Mekong for millennia, but their self-consciousness as a people is not so old. Angkorian kings, looking for a glorious Indian heritage, claimed Kambu and Kaundinya as mythic ancestors, but ordinary Khmers probably looked no further than their village with its clan ancestors and local legends. We have no idea when and how they, as distinct from their rulers, began to think of themselves as Khmers. Probably history had a lot to do with the process, with Khmer-ness defining itself against those who were not-Khmer. In the earliest times this was the Cham kingdoms along the central Vietnamese coast, later the Siamese and Vietnamese. The Khmer sometimes fought them and sometimes married them, and all became Cambodian.

Cambodia's history began while the Caesars ruled Rome, but its political borders are surprisingly modern. Just how modern can be seen in a group of statues on the southern slope of Wat Phnom, the hill that is

A Cambodian monk
arranges his robe at the
9th-century temple of
Preah Vihear.

the symbolic navel of Phnom Penh, where three goddesses bring offerings to a golden *chakravartin*, the righteous world conqueror of Buddhist
mythology. The foremost, bare breasted and wearing a triple crown, bears a
miniature temple, the second a lotus bloom and the third the rod of royal
authority. They represent the three provinces of Siem Reap, Sisophon and
Battambang, and the monarch is King Sisowath, who ruled between 1904
and 1927. To Sisowath's right a soldier waves an enormous French flag, and
an inscription on a plaque commemorates the occasion, the Franco-Siamese
treaty of 1907. The three provinces had been lost to Siam – the old name
for Thailand – in the late 18th century and Sisowath regarded their return
as the greatest triumph of his reign. The story was not to end there, for in
1941 the Japanese forced France to give them back to Bangkok, and it was

only in 1946 that both sides agreed on the present border. Even then the Thais continued to occupy the Angkorian cliff-top temple of Preah Vihear overlooking the Cambodian plain, until the International Court of Justice confirmed Cambodia's ownership in 2013.

The border with Vietnam is equally recent and even more contentious, for the Mekong delta was absorbed by Vietnam in the 17th and 18th centuries, and a substantial Khmer population still lives there (the Khmer lands of Vietnam are known as Kampuchea Krom, 'lower Cambodia'). In the late 19th century the French drew an administrative boundary between Cambodian and Vietnamese territory, but successive Cambodian kings never accepted it as a national border, and as recently as 1949 King Sihanouk petitioned the French National Assembly for Kampuchea Krom's return. A border treaty was signed in 1985, but the location of border markers continues to be a highly sensitive issue in Cambodian politics.

SROK KHMER

Casual visitors can easily form the impression that Cambodia is composed of villages, rice fields and orchards, with the jungle reduced to disciplined

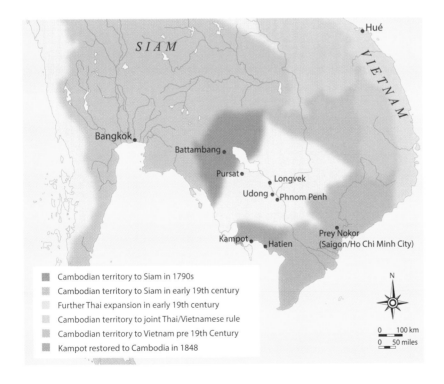

Cambodian territory to Siam in 1790s
Cambodian territory to Siam in early 19th century
Further Thai expansion in early 19th century
Cambodian territory to joint Thai/Vietnamese rule
Cambodian territory to Vietnam pre 19th Century
Kampot restored to Cambodia in 1848

LEFT
Changes to Cambodia's borders between the late 18th and early 20th centuries.

copses or an occasional view of hills. The impression is misleading, for Cambodia's history was played out over a landscape that was heavily forested. 'Only here and there, beside the rivers or within the interior, around a few rice fields, there have sprung up groups of wretched huts,' wrote explorer Henri Mouhot in the 1850s. This was true well into living memory, as in this record of an outing to a pepper plantation near Kampot around 1954:

We took the same road leading to Kep [and] *turned left at a fork onto a dirt road leading into the jungle ... The road took us through many Cambodian villages, then finally led us deep into the jungle* [where it] *narrowed down to a mere path so we abandoned jeep and made our way on foot.* [We were] *told by our host that this part of the jungle was thickly populated by tigers and wild boars...*

ABOVE
Henri Mouhot, the mid-19th century French explorer who made Cambodia known to a wide public.

The host may have been exaggerating to give his visitors a frisson, but the tigers certainly existed, along with elephants, rhinos, deer and buffalo.

In historical terms Cambodia has been very sparsely populated. In 1950 there were less than four and a half million people and in 1875 under one million. Figures before that are largely guesswork, although the city of Angkor at its height may have accommodated three quarters of a million people. Population density was correspondingly very low, and this has meant that those who wished not to be governed – tribal peoples, and bandits and rebels – could always find jungles and hills where they could escape the reach of kings and governments. Also not to be overlooked is the role of the wilderness in providing 'forest products', the kingfisher feathers, rhino horn, ivory, medicinal barks and magical herbs that for over 2,000 years were the backbone of Cambodia's economic dealings with the world.

Most Cambodians, for most of their history, have been fishermen and farmers, yet Cambodia's soils are among the poorest in all tropical Asia. The country's great good fortune, the source of its rice fields and fisheries and its very existence, is the annual flooding of the Mekong River. During the rainy season the river rises so high at Phnom Penh that the downstream channels cannot handle the volume, and the water begins to back up into the

Tonle Sap, which is both a river and a lake (the name means 'big freshwater river'). The combined river and lake are essentially a huge back-swamp. As the floodwater flows in it triples in size, until the flooded zone extends as far as 50km (31 miles) from the dry-season shoreline; then, as the rains end the water recedes, leaving behind an immense load of fertile, mineral-rich silt.

Around the swamps are alluvial plains that flood in the rainy season, backed by low terraces that rarely or never flood. When rice farming first came to Cambodia it could be practised wherever the land was flat enough, but in the flood-free zone repeated cropping eventually lowered soil fertility to a level from which it could never recover. Only where annual floods replenished the soil could rice be grown for century after century. This rice-growing zone, running north-west from the Vietnamese border to the western end of the Tonle Sap Lake and with a northern spur up the Mekong as far as Kratie, is the stage on which Cambodian history was played out, but it makes up only two-thirds of the kingdom.

THE RHYTHM OF LIFE

The true heroes of Cambodia are its farmers and fishermen. Kings and armies could not have existed without them, and the rhythm of their lives is still much the same today as it has been for millennia.

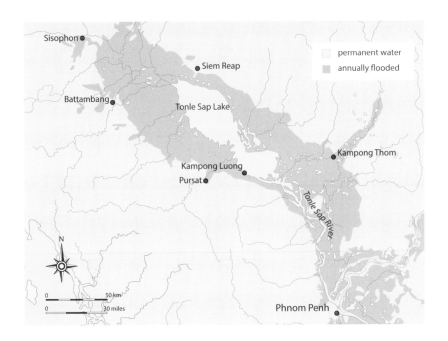

LEFT
Annually inundated area of the Tonle Sap/Mekong floodplain – the zone suitable for wet rice and dense population.

ABOVE

Major rice-growing regions of modern Cambodia.

Cambodian farmers are simple folk, but farming is immensely sophisticated. The farmer has to know when to plant, what to plant, how to manage soils and pests, and how to approach the spirits that inhabit the landscape. Farming is also hard work, and yet it has poetry – the many strains of rice, for example, have evocative names such as white cat, red cat, parrot's eyebrow, rattan spike and serpent's neck, each with its own characteristics.

Rice is grown in rain-fed plots marked out by small mud walls, or bunds, which hold the water in place, while an underlying clay layer prevents it from draining away into the sandy subsoil. Seedlings are raised in nursery beds at the beginning of the rainy season and planted out to the fields in August/ September as the rains end. The operation is highly labour intensive, taking 30–40 person-hours to set out 1ha (2.5 acres). The plants grow in the standing water until the ears appear and begin to ripen, when the bunds are broken open and the fields drained. This is followed by harvesting and threshing from December to February, another period of frantic work.

Nature is capricious. In the decade of the 1990s there were floods in 1991, a drought in June 1994 and a flood in July, a flood in 1996, a typhoon followed by a drought in 1997/98, and in 1999 floods in July–August and again in November. This is one hazard of the farming. Another is finance.

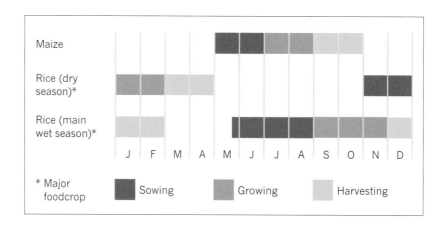

RIGHT

Cambodian crop calendar.

Cambodian farmers are perennially short of cash and have to take out loans against future harvests, and in the absence of efficient banks the village moneylender (often Chinese) has for centuries been an unpleasant fact of life on a par with drought and floods and just as unavoidable.

The basic farming unit is the family. In the middle of the 20th century the average farm family in Cambodia was made up of 5–6 people, farmed 2–3ha (5–7.4 acres), and ate two-thirds of what it grew. Contrary to what the Khmer Rouge claimed, inequality was minimal and there was no class of rich landowners to oppress the poor (the village moneylender was not a landowner).

The traditional Cambodian plough is made of wood, and only rarely carries a metal plough-tip. The reason for this is not down to backwardness but to practicality: the layer of fertile clay is shallow, and a robust metal plough would puncture it and bring up the sandy subsoil. This apparently nonchalant approach to farming has led to a belief among the neighbours of the Khmer that they are lazy and ignorant. 'The people do not know the

17

RIGHT
*Vast areas of Cambodia are
flooded during the rainy
season.*

proper way to grow food,' complained a 19th-century Vietnamese emperor. 'They use mattocks and hoes, but no oxen...' Perhaps the emperor was misinformed, or maybe the Khmer farmers he was familiar with had been through hard times, but in both modern and ancient Cambodia the fields have been ploughed with cows or buffalo, and today motorized tillers are becoming increasingly popular.

The average yield on Cambodian rice land today is just over a ton a hectare, the lowest in Southeast Asia, although in southern Battambang it can be as high as two or three tons. The Mekong delta in Vietnam has yields more than double this. On the other hand, due to low population density the Cambodian farmer needs yields of only 25 per cent of those of Vietnam to feed the same or a larger number of people. Farmers normally raise only one crop a year. Zhou Daguan, a medieval Chinese visitor to Angkor, reported four, but he might have meant multiple crops of different types in different seasons (floating, flood recession, bunded wet rice, swidden), rather than four consecutive crops in one field.

Fishing provides the other great staple of Cambodian life. Fishing is more democratic than rice farming, as flooded rice fields, ponds, irrigation ditches and streams are open to everyone and very little capital is needed. It is often a part-time occupation combined with farming, and provides protein (almost twice as much as cattle, pigs and chickens combined), insurance against crop disaster and a source of income.

The huge flood zone of the Tonle Sap provides three-quarters of

LEFT
Fish is a central source of food for the rural poor due to its abundance and availability, and contributes greatly to national food security.

Cambodia's annual inland fish catch and 60 per cent of the country's protein intake, and fishing, fish-processing, marketing and gear making are the primary occupation of a third of the population and the secondary occupation of half. The Tonle Sap lake and river are the world's most productive inland fishery, yet the lake is vulnerable: it depends on the annual floods to refresh its nutrients, and on the continued health of the flooded forests around its edges where the fish spawn. It is also vulnerable to overfishing: catches have fallen by 50–70 per cent in the past decade, and the composition has changed from large to more small species, which is an indication of overfishing. Fishermen respond by investing in higher technology gear, which allows them to keep up in the short term but builds problems for the future.

VILLAGES AND CITIES

Eight out of every 10 Cambodians live in villages. There is probably no such thing as a typical village, but they can be broadly divided between those in the fertile land of the 'zone of settlement' and those outside it. Prek Por on the bank of the Mekong in Kampong Cham province, a little north of Phnom Penh, in one of the most fertile and thickly settled areas of the country, can be taken to represent the first group.

A sociologist studying Prek Por in the mid-1960s counted 4,500 inhabitants living in 1,500 households spread over 12 hamlets. The people were well off and relatively well educated. Everyone had enough to eat, most households owned their own land (private land ownership was an

ABOVE

The Cambodian village community centres around the Buddhist monastery.

BELOW

A shrine for a neak ta, a protective village spirit who serves as the 'ancestor' of all the village.

innovation introduced by the French in the colonial period, to much opposition), and almost everyone could read Khmer.

The villagers' sense of belonging was not based on the village, or the hamlets, but on the three village monasteries. Households chose one of the three as 'theirs' and attended its festivals and sponsored its monks and projects, and the monks in return would visit 'their' households on their morning alms rounds. Households would send their boy children to the monks for the obligatory term as novices, and the monks in return would provide the necessary rituals for births, weddings, funerals and the gaining of merit. Monastic Buddhism, in short, provided the centre of Khmer community life. In earlier ages the monasteries had provided medical and banking facilities, architectural assistance and other social services. However, as part of the advance of secular modernity since the beginning of the 20th century, the government took over more and more of these, and by 1966 the monasteries' only such role was in providing a basic education to village boys during their terms as novices.

The study from which this is taken does not mention religion at a level below the monastery, which is a pity, as a great deal takes place in the household. The house contains the shrines of the ancestors, who are present and very much active in the lives of the living through dreams and ritual. It also contains the shrine of the household goddess and of the *tevoda*, the divine messengers who provide a direct link between the household and the gods. The monastery, in short, is only one part of religious life, which centres around the household and the family as much as the Buddhist community.

The study also does not mention the shrine of the *neak ta*, the spirit owner of the village. It plays just as important a role as the monastery in drawing the community together, and its origins can probably be traced back to the clan shrines of the prehistoric period. Add to this the cast of minor spirits that inhabit the village and its fields, and you have a rich and fecund supernatural world that coexists with the human one.

Prek Por was not physically isolated, but it did not have much contact with the outside world. Jeeps could travel along the riverbank and a few inland tracks, but it was unusual to see one. There was no bus service. The Mekong was the sole practical means for travelling long distances. Kampong Cham town and Phnom Penh were each several hours away by ferry, but passengers never got off at Prek Por (why should they?), so there was no interchange with the city or the provincial capital unless a villager made the effort, or unless someone from the city – like a merchant, relative or official – came to visit. Today there are more and better roads, and bus services, cars and motorbikes, but Prek Por in the 1960s was only halfway emerged from the Cambodia of centuries ago.

This was, and is, the village that visitors think of as typically Cambodian. Beyond the fertile zone there was quite a different reality. Michael Vickery, who wrote extensively on both ancient Cambodia and the modern era, has given an evocative description of a visit to an isolated village near the Thai border just a few years before our sociologist was studying Prek Por. The meaning of 'isolated' can be judged by his description of the journey: the first 30km (19 miles) from the main road took half an hour, the next 30km took an hour, and the final 30km took two hours across a moonscape of dried-out paddy fields and crumbling field bunds.

No rain had fallen for three years. There were no schools and no clinics, and the villagers met Vickery and his companions with scarcely concealed hostility. There was a marked absence of the hospitality that our sociologist found at Prek Por. The villagers did not like city people, because the city meant nothing but trouble. Yet their life was far from miserable, or even impoverished. Because of the drought there was no rice, but there were chickens and pigs in the village, and tubers and vegetables in the forest, and boys hunted lizards in the dry fields. The villagers had silkworms and wove and dyed their own silk, but when Vickery asked if they would sell him some they refused, for the nearest market was 25km (16 miles) away and there was nothing in it that they wanted. They had nothing to ask for from the government and everything to fear, and the forest was a source of food and a refuge to which they could decamp if danger threatened.

At the opposite pole to the villages were

BELOW
Phnom Penh in the 19th century.

the cities. Cambodia has had urban settlements for more than 2,000 years, although the exact nature and function of the very earliest ones is debated. Phnom Penh became the capital of modern Cambodia in 1866, but it traces its history back to the early 15th century and is undoubtedly older. As centres of royal power and wealth, urban settlements were fought over and periodically destroyed. Henri Mouhot, passing through Phnom Penh on his way to Angkor in the mid-19th century, described it as a single straggling street of merchants, with boats lining the riverbank ready for a quick escape if danger threatened. With good reason: since 1834 Phnom Penh has been burnt by the Siamese, burnt again in 1861 by rebels, attacked by anti-French insurgents in 1885 and evacuated by the Khmer Rouge in 1975. As recently as 1997 there were tanks in the streets as rival factions battled it out.

SOCIETY

At the centre of Cambodian society is the family, and all relationships, family-like, are vertical. To use Khmer terminology, the organizing principle is the *khsae*, or 'string'. As a child the Khmer learns that he has a certain place in the family, owing obedience to those above him (parents and elders), and demanding the same from those below him (younger siblings). As an adult he transposes these relationships to the wider world, seeking favours and protection from a patron who stands in the position of parent in return for loyalty and obedience, and simultaneously standing as a patron himself for those below him. Life outside the *khsae*, which is to say life as a free agent, would be impossible and is therefore inconceivable. It follows that society functions on the basis of loyalty and favours given by one party in the expectation of future benefits from the other in return. In Western eyes this is nepotism and bribery, but Cambodians find the Western way of doing things cold and impersonal.

The would-be patron advertises his ability to dispense favours through the public display of his wealth and his closeness to those even more powerful than himself. Patronage-based societies are therefore societies of conspicuous display, which the outsider can mistake for conspicuous consumption. It is patronage, rather than simply vulgar ostentation, that lies behind the top-range BMWs and Mercedes ranked outside Phnom Penh's best restaurants, the multi-balconied villas behind high walls in the best suburbs, and the bling-laden weddings displayed to the world on social media.

The pioneering 19th-century sociologist Max Weber distinguished between 'rational' or 'legal' states and 'patrimonial' states. The first two are modern Western liberal democracies in which authority derives from law, and bureaucrats and politicians must disregard personal relationships; the second are traditional autocracies in which the state is the inheritance (patrimony) of the ruler. In the patrimonial state all law proceeds from the ruler, all positions of authority are his to delegate, and there is no guarantee of personal rights or the security of property. The patrimonial state can be efficient as a form of government, but it is the enemy of liberalism and democracy.

In the 20th century, Weber's concept has been redefined as neo-patrimonialism, an intellectual category introduced to explain post-colonial states in which liberal democracy has failed to flourish. The neo-patrimonial state preserves the institutions of democracy (elections, legislatures), but power is exercised through traditional patron-client relationships.

Every state needs to establish its authority, meaning the story it tells to justify its use of power. Force alone will rarely work for long. In the 'rational' modern state, authority rests ultimately on the idea that all citizens participate in government and that it ultimately reflects the common will and interest. Inequality and injustice are therefore resented and can undermine authority. In the patrimonial state, on the contrary, inequality is accepted as the outward sign of the patron's ability to deliver benefits, and one man's injustice is another's justice.

KINGSHIP

Cambodia has been a patrimonial society from the very beginning. This is hardly surprising: patrimonialism is rooted in the family, and continues as a clear undertone in even the most modern of modern liberal democracies.

In 1863, the apex of the Cambodian state was occupied by King Norodom, 'grand king with divine feet, superior to anyone, descendant of the deities and of Vishnu'. Around him was the court, including powerful individuals such as the Queen Mother and the *obbareach* (a position often translated as Second King), other members of the royal family, a cabinet of ministers who served at the pleasure of the ruler, and various formal and informal advisors, not least those representing Norodom's suzerain, the King of Siam.

Serving the king were the 'mandarins', as the French called them, under the misapprehension that Cambodian officials could be compared to the

BELOW
The Second King of Cambodia (the future King Norodom, reigned 1860–1904), from Henri Mouhot's Travels in the Central Parts of Indochina.

professional bureaucracy of the Vietnamese state they had just conquered. Those in the palace alone numbered in the hundreds, far more than were strictly needed, because patronage demanded rewards – in other words, official positions were make-work posts created so that clients could have titles and robes. Outside the capital were 56 provinces, each with its governor and mandarins mirroring the centre, each individual the apex of his own personal *khsae*. The official posts carried very little in the way of salary, but the officials did not actually expect salaries – what they wanted was the opportunity to extort charges. For example, when a judge heard a case, the custom was to impose a fine by way of punishment, of which one-third went to the plaintiff, one-third to the king and one-third to the judge. Unsurprisingly, official positions were valued for what they could bring in, and bought and sold accordingly.

The French considered Norodom an Oriental despot, but his authority was hemmed in on every side by the very system that supported him, for while kingship was respected the king was not. Everyone, from the *obbareach* to the smallest provincial judge, was prepared to transfer allegiance at the first opportunity. A French observer described how the *khsae* fostered chronic instability:

> *Left to itself,* [Cambodia] *will immediately fall into complete anarchy. ... No middle class exists ... There are only the mandarins who do not work, and a miserable population* [which is] *exploited to the extreme. ... The class of mandarins, two or three times more numerous than necessary, can only be partly satisfied by the king. ... The result is a genuinely unattached party ... ready to throw itself into the arms of the first pretender that shows up, under the condition that the latter promises, in the case of success, to make tabula rasa and to hand to his friends the exclusive right to exploit Cambodia.* (Doudart de Lagree, quoted in Gregor Muller, *Colonial Cambodia's 'Bad Frenchmen'*)

THE PERSISTENCE OF THE PAST

The French set out to reform the kingdom but found themselves blocked at every step by Norodom, who could understand no alternative to the *khsae*. Ultimately, the French took over the state themselves. Their motives, of course, were mixed, and in some areas the efforts were non-existent

(education for Cambodians being a major absence), but when they granted Cambodia the bare bones of independence they provided a constitution, an elected legislative assembly, a free press and political parties in possession of distinctive political platforms. Cambodia, in short, was brought into the modern world as a liberal democracy.

Patrimony reasserted itself from the very beginning. It seemed that no one understood the principles involved, and perhaps no one, or almost no one, did. The one notable exception, Cambodia's first democratically elected prime minister, died shortly after taking office, and no individual of his stature was available to replace him. This perhaps justifies the Great Man theory of history: if India had not had Nehru, it might have followed the same path. Cambodia had no such good fortune.

Sihanouk, Lon Nol, the Khmer Rouge and UNTAC have each hunted for a shortcut to modernity, and in the process the patrimonial and the rational legal state have become ever more deeply entangled. The neo-patrimonial state has turned out to be far stronger than the patrimonial state, for the tools of bureaucracy and the mass party allow it to reach into people's lives and exercise control in a way that Norodom could never imagine possible.

The Economist Intelligence Unit publishes an annual Democracy Index measuring the state of democracy around the globe, and in February 2018 it downgraded Cambodia from a 'hybrid regime' (one with a mix of democratic and authoritarian structures) to an authoritarian one. One way of interpreting this is as the failure of a wrong-headed attempt to impose an alien facade on a centuries-old social and political system. Another is that it represents the personal failure of the country's current leadership – the man or the system. No doubt there is an element of truth in both interpretations, but history never ends.

ABOVE

Cambodia has had a number of consitutions since independence from France in 1953. None has brought it true democracy.

RULE OF LAW

The World Justice Project publishes annual reports measuring the rule of law across eight factors, namely constraints on government power, absence of corruption, open government, fundamental rights, order and security, regulatory enforcement, civil justice and criminal justice (see *https://worldjusticeproject. org/sites/default/files/documents/WJP_ROLI_2017-* *18_Online-Edition_0.pdf*). In 2017/18, Cambodia's overall rank was 112 out of 113 countries surveyed, with a score of 0.32 (scores are from zero to 1). On constraints on government power, the factor most closely related to patrimonial rule, it ranked 110; and 113 on corruption and open government.

2

FOUNDATIONS
Before Cambodia
Prehistory to the 8th century AD

In 1962, Elman Service, an American anthropologist, proposed four general categories for classifying human societies: bands, tribes, chiefdoms and states. This theoretical framework is still widely used, and although modern scholars are wary of applying it in a rigidly evolutionary sense, it provides a useful guideline for the way societies developed in Cambodia.

OPPOSITE
*Part of Isanapura,
a pre-Angkorian city.*

BELOW
*As societies develop from
bands to states they steadily
grow in size and complexity.*

BANDS

Margaret Thatcher famously said that there was no such thing as society. The English philosopher Thomas Hobbes looked back to 'a time of Warre, where every man is Enemy to every man', and declared that life in the wild was 'solitary, poor, nasty, brutish and short'. Hobbes believed that the individual was the basic social unit, but the French philosopher Jean-Jacques Rousseau felt that the force of sexual attraction meant it should be found in the nuclear family. Mrs Thatcher would agree with both, but nowhere have anthropologists discovered humans living either alone or in nuclear families, and all the evidence is that the irreducible human unit is Service's hunter-gatherer band of a few dozen related individuals.

The fact that the band's members are related is significant. The band doubtless provides safety and sex for its members, but it also passes on vital

Membership	Number of people	Settlement pattern	Basis of relationships	Ethnicities and languages
band	dozens	mobile	kin	1
tribe	hundreds	mobile or fixed: 1 or more villages	kin, descent groups	1
chiefdom	thousands	fixed: 1 or more villages	kin, rank and residence	1
state	tens of thousands	fixed: many villages and cities	class and residence	1 or more

knowledge such as how to make spears and hunt game, which mushrooms are edible and which are best avoided, and the names of the gods and their proper ceremonies. With so much vital knowledge to pass on it makes sense to have as many people as possible involved in the upbringing of children. It also makes sense that these people should be blood relatives, since humans, like other animals from ants to blue whales, are genetically programmed to look after their own.

Older members of the band have greater authority than younger ones, men hold formal authority over women, and the opinions of individuals with greater than average foresight, persuasiveness or hunting skills will be listened to with more respect than those of their less gifted peers, but after making allowances for all this, bands are democratic, and leadership by an individual, or a group of elite individuals, is absent. Decision making is typically the result of long discussion, and is delivered in the form, 'It would be good if it were done', rather than 'Do it!'

Bands are poor but equal. Everyone has the same stone and wooden tools, eats the same food, and dresses, if at all, in the same leaves or animal skins. If the band has any property it would be its territory, the piece of land across which it hunts animals and collects forest products, but modern foragers think more in terms of themselves belonging to the land than of the land belonging to them. The basic moral rule in such a society is not 'Thou shalt not steal', but 'Thou shalt share', since a failure to share threatens the very survival of the group.

Living in bands is not easy. Conflicts arise, most often between men and concerning women, but also over food sharing and through the simple clash of personalities. With no one in a position of authority, the only solution to serious disputes is violence or a split in the band along family lines.

TRIBES

The next of Service's four categories is the tribe, formed when societies develop ways of vastly expanding their production of food so that they become able to settle down in villages (not all tribes are sedentary, of course, but in Cambodia they were). Unlike bands, they can support populations of hundreds of people, while large tribes can spread across multiple villages with thousands of members.

New forms of social integration are necessary for societies of this size, and kinship is replaced by large, kin-based clans with a common ancestor and united around a clan shrine or temple, where clan leaders serve as priests and priestesses, and common religious ceremonies are held. This was not, of course, the full extent of Neolithic religion, but it was an important aspect, for out of it would eventually develop the sacred character of Cambodian kings.

Tribal elders typically form a council of village elders, but while the elders have great prestige they lack authority and are unable to enforce decisions. In larger and wealthier tribes, 'big men' may emerge, working for years to build up a stock of pigs and other high-value items that they will then give away in large formal feasts. These displays mean that they might be listened to with a little more respect in the village council, but do not translate into leadership or authority. Tribes, like bands, are essentially leaderless.

CHIEFDOMS

The third of Service's four categories, chiefdoms, form when the ephemeral rivalries of tribal big men are resolved into permanent full-time leaders possessing real power and authority.

The office of chief, unlike that of the elder or big man, is hereditary. Around and supporting him is an equally hereditary elite, made up of families and lineages connected to him by blood and ranked by their genealogical closeness to him. The elite shares the chief's prestige and authority, and its status is frequently signalled by special costumes, titles and forms of address that set it apart from the rest of the villagers, who can be called commoners. The chief and the elite will not engage in agriculture, which is left to the commoners.

Chiefs control trade, especially in prestige luxury goods such as exotic beads, fine pottery and metalwork. They also extract taxes from the commoners in the form of food, cloth and ceramics, much of which is redistributed through gift giving and ritual feasting in the style of big men, but enough remains to ensure that they enjoy a high standard of living in keeping with their status. The evidence that a society has made the transition from tribe to chiefdom shows up in the archaeological record in post-holes signalling the presence of some houses that are significantly larger than the majority, certain graves showing a larger quantity and richer range of grave offerings than others, and skeletal remains, which can show quite clearly the results of a life of better than average nutrition.

Chiefdoms are better at war than tribes. They are better because they are bigger, but also because some of their members can specialize in being warriors. The warriors are, by definition, young males, and they find warfare on the chief's behalf attractive partly because of the opportunity for plunder, but even more because it offers the chance to win renown and to carry off the opponents' women. Warfare tends to become especially acute following the introduction of metals, usually in the order first bronze then iron. The arrival of iron in particular triggers an outbreak of intensified warfare, just as the arrival of gunpowder weapons will do at a much later point.

Chiefdoms are not entirely parasitic. Societies led by chiefs respond more quickly to emergencies and, through the redistribution of wealth, can cushion the less fortunate in times of adversity. This redistributive function forms the basis of chiefly paternalism – the chief is father to all his people, no matter how distant or even non-existent the actual blood relationship. Chiefdoms are also able to form and execute plans that will enrich everyone– which is to say, raiding and trading. Most significantly, the chief, backed by the gods and ancestors, can enforce an end to disputes between members of the tribe. It might seem paradoxical given their war-prone nature, but chiefdoms bring about an increase in peace and security, at least for their own members.

Chiefdoms are also states of mind, and as such they develop foundation myths that explain how chiefs rule because the gods will it. Surprisingly often, these myths tell how the chiefly family and entire elites have external origins, the point presumably being to emphasize that they belong to something bigger than the world of the commoners.

Chiefdoms can have populations of tens or even hundreds of thousands, and can develop into complex constellations of societies with lesser chiefs who recognize the supreme authority of a paramount leader.

STATES

States first arose in Mesopotamia and Egypt around 5,500 years ago, slightly later in India and China, and later still in Mesoamerica and the central-west coast of South America. Each was independent of the others, implying that some general principle was at work, and a popular explanation put forward in 1970 by Robert Carneiro, curator of the American Museum of Natural History, suggests that the crucial preconditions were high population density and a circumscribed fertile area.

The catalyst was war. Raiding for food and women had been present from the earliest tribal period (for that matter, it was quite common in band-level hunter-gatherer societies). However, at that period, those on the losing side could always flee deeper into the jungle to escape their enemies – one patch of land, after all, was much like another. But where the supply of land was limited this eventually ceased to be an option. Under these circumstances, the leaders of warrior bands no longer grabbed what they could and went home – they took the land itself. Those on the losing side faced reduction to tributary status, enslavement or extermination, while chiefdoms grew larger and larger and their number smaller and smaller.

The possession of larger populations and territories produced profound changes in those who survived. Agriculture remained the basis of wealth, but trade became increasingly important and wide ranging. Writing and numeracy developed, and a middle class emerged made up of craftsmen and traders engaged in producing and procuring luxury goods for the elite and bureaucrats skilled in the arts of administration. Religion differentiated into the state religion of the elite and the common religion of the cultivators, with specialized architecture for the gods. Village settlements become centres for trading, administration and religious ritual, at which point they could be called cities, a term signifying role rather than size. This steadily increasing sophistication allowed states to grow far larger than chiefdoms, becoming kingdoms and empires.

BEFORE HISTORY IN CAMBODIA: LAANG SPEAN

Laang Spean, the Cave of Bridges, sits at the top of an isolated limestone hill on the road from Battambang to Pailin called Phnom Teak Treang. Hills like this, *phnom* in Khmer, are traditionally the home of supernatural beings, so it is fitting that Phnom Teak Treang should have been the home of the first

RIGHT

*Phnom Teak Trang and the
cave of Laang Spean.*

RIGHT

*Phnom Teak Trang and the
cave of Laang Spean.*

Cambodians. The oldest identifiably human finds at Laang Spean are a few flaked stone tools dating to around 70,000 years ago, but in the absence of skeletal remains it is impossible to say whether these were the work of *Homo sapiens* or some other humanoid species that made the move into Asia ahead of us. If they are indeed evidence of anatomically modern humans it would be a momentous discovery, as the oldest currently known sign of our ancestors in mainland Southeast Asia is a partial cranium from Tam Pa Ling ('Monkey Cave') in Laos, dated to 46,000–63,000 years ago.

Next come stone tools dated to 5,000–11,000 years ago. These belong to the Hoabinhian culture, found throughout mainland Southeast Asia and into southern China and northern Sumatra. No skeletal remains have been found with the tools, but Hoabinhians have been discovered elsewhere in Asia and we can be sure that the people who left these were modern humans. Their genes could well be present in modern Cambodians.

From the top of their hill, the Hoabinhians of Laang Spean would have looked out over a wide plain of mixed forest and grassland, flooded during the rainy season, arid and dusty during the dry season. The land teemed with wild deer, pigs, monkeys, porcupines and pangolins (animals that look like miniature armour-plated dinosaurs), as well as more dangerous creatures including rhinoceroses, tigers and leopards. The Hoabinhians hunted almost all of them, but three-quarters of the bones in the cave come from just two animals, the gaur, described as 'a water buffalo on steroids', and the banteng, smaller but still large enough to be dangerous. Both species favour open forests with areas of grassland. The hunters probably set fires at the start of the rainy season to burn off scrub and start new growth to attract the cattle, which could then be driven into the marshes along the nearby river, where their size and weight would have made them vulnerable.

It is most unlikely that the band stayed at Laang Spean year-round. There are still a few Southeast Asian hunter-gatherers in the mountains of the Philippines and the jungles of peninsular Malaysia, and they live in caves or rock shelters during the wet season, and travel through the forests during the dry season, spending just a few nights in any one place. The dry-season camps are extremely simple affairs of branches and bark, and leave almost no impression on the landscape. The sheer difficulty of finding them is the single major reason why archaeologists are so dependent on what they freely admit to be the highly skewed collections of remains buried in the floors of caves.

BELOW
The excavations at Laang Spean, conducted annually in the winter months.

Modern bands split or merge as food supplies wax and wane, or as conflicts create tensions or opportunities. Bands with adjacent territories normally speak mutually intelligible languages and are closely interrelated. The Laang Spean band would have married its women into, and taken its own women from, neighbouring bands like these, a practice that has the advantage of strengthening bonds and defusing tensions between neighbouring bands. As a result, prehistoric Cambodia, and all Southeast Asia, formed a giant mosaic of tiny interrelated hunter-gatherer bands.

The forest provided wood, bamboo, rattan and vines to make baskets and snares, and fruit, tubers, birds' eggs and honey for food. This is the 'gathering' side of the hunter-gatherer lifestyle, and it brings into focus elements of the Stone Age lifestyle that are easily overlooked. Honey, for example, is one of the favourite foods of modern foragers, so much so that falling out of trees accounts for a high proportion of deaths. This continues to the present day – in modern Cambodia falls rank thirty-fifth as a cause of death, between heart disease and peptic ulcers.

The absence of fish bones at Laang Spean lends weight to the impression that these people were not eating fish. This is rather a puzzle, given the abundance of fish in the nearby Sangke River. Stone Age Cambodians presumably had canoes and/or rafts, and/or fishing lines and traps, but no shell or bone fish hooks have been found, and no weights for nets (thrown nets need weights around the edges to make them spread out and sink). Nor is there evidence of domesticated crops or domesticated animals – not even dogs.

Did they wear clothes? This might seem a pointless question to ask on the hot and humid Cambodian plains, but at the beginning of the Laang Spean period the Ice Age was just ending and the climate was much cooler than it is today, and in any case even modern Cambodians find the nights cold in around December and January. Clothes do not survive for thousands of years, so how can we tell? Data from modern hunter-gatherer societies shows that people living where the coldest month averages below -10°C (14°F) typically cover about 80 per cent of the body, after which there is a rapid fall-off to almost, but not quite complete, nakedness at around 20°C (68°F). Today's January minimum temperature in much of Cambodia is around 20°C, so it seems probable that the ancient Laang Spean people went (almost) naked for most of the year, but may have rugged up (slightly) for the winter. If they did they left no needles, and therefore did no sewing.

In any case, people who live in parts of the world where clothing is not strictly needed still find body paint, tattooing and other forms of personal adornment useful for ritual purposes. We can be reasonably sure that Laang Spean's occupants had a rich ritual life involving music, dance and ceremonies, but we have no means of knowing anything about it.

What of their religious beliefs? In the absence of burials and artefacts we have no way of knowing about these, but foragers as a general rule do not have a concept of a high (supreme) god who dictates morality and intervenes in the world. What they do have is a generalized belief in 'animal spirits', meaning that a life force (which is the meaning of *anima*) permeates everything, from humans and other animals, to trees, rocks and mountains. Just as important in terms of social evolution is what they do not have: no temples, altars, priests or other marks of institutionalized religion. These typically begin with the invention of farming and settled village life.

THE NEOLITHIC PERIOD

Farming was invented twice in the Old World, in the Middle East, where it involved wheat, barley, cattle and sheep, and independently in East Asia, where rice and millet were domesticated along with cattle, pigs and dogs.

Rice was originally a swamp grass with varieties native to every continent except Antarctica. It was probably first domesticated in the middle and lower Yangtze valley in around 6,500–4,500 BC, before the technology

THE CIRCLES OF MEMOT

The mysterious earthworks of the Memotian culture straddle the border with Vietnam in the east of Cambodia. More than 55 circles have been identified. They are 150–300m (492–984ft) across and follow a nearly identical plan, with a circular earth platform in the centre, a circular ditch around that, and a steep earth embankment enclosing both ditch and platform. Openings in the outer embankment seem to have given access to the central area via a wooden bridge over the ditch.

The embankments do not seem to be defensive, nor were they capable of holding water, which rules out their use as reservoirs for irrigating crops. The current best guess is that they were used to pen animals with the help of wooden palisades on top of the embankment. They span roughly 2,000 years, 2300–300 BC, from before the arrival of the first rice farmers to the time when the first towns were emerging in the delta. No non-Memotian pottery has been found inside the villages, and Memotian pots never turn up at non-Memotian sites.

The museum in Memot town has a large diorama of a circle in its heyday, showing animals in the ditch, farmers and herders going about their business, and a circle of bamboo houses very like those used by today's tribal minority in the highlands of the north-east.

spread to Southeast Asia and the Indian subcontinent. There is no totally satisfactory explanation as to why this happened after tens of thousands of years of hunting and gathering – no doubt the end of the Ice Age was the crucial enabling factor, but people could have kept on foraging indefinitely. Possibly an answer lies in competitive feasting, the apparently universal wish of humans to impress friends and neighbours by sharing food as bountifully as possible, making farming an accidental result of the wish to keep up with the Stone Age Joneses.

The first rice required very little care, but as farmers devoted more and more attention to their larders they began to manage the swamps by creating artificial flooded fields. Flooded rice fields produce methane, and a sharp rise in global methane in around 3000 BC would seem to date the transition to intensive cultivation. Populations surged, and soon the rice farmers had occupied all the suitable land in the middle and lower Yangtze and began to move southwards. First they colonized Yunnan and Guizhou, then – beginning about 2200 BC – they spread very rapidly across mainland Southeast Asia from northern Thailand to the Mekong delta.

Rice provided the basis for settled life in villages and for rapid population increases, but settling down is bad for your health, at least in its early stages. Everywhere in the world the first farmers caught diseases from their livestock (measles from cattle, influenza from ducks, plague from rats), narrowed their diet and therefore suffered from dietary deficiencies, and set up a cycle of infestation by parasitic worms when they used excrement for fertilizer. Why, given these drawbacks, did farming replace foraging? A study from the mountains of the Philippines island of Luzon suggests an answer. Luzon is the home of a modern hunter-gather people called the Agta, and some of them have recently taken up farming at the urging of their government. The settled Agta have higher morbidity and mortality (worse health and higher death rates) than their non-farming kin, and more of their children die in infancy.

This would seem like an excellent set of reasons for going back to the forest, but the settled Agta do enjoy one significant advantage over hunter-gatherers: they have more babies. The reasons for this are not clear, but having more babies results in, despite higher infant death rates, the farmers having more children who survive to an age when they can have children of their own. On a worldwide basis the invention of farming saw the rate of population growth increase from less than 0.001 per cent a year (hunter-gatherers) to around 0.04 per cent (farmers). Over time – an extremely long time, so long that the hunter-gatherers would not have been aware it was happening – the farmers out-populated the hunter-gatherers.

The farmers probably spoke ancestral forms of the Austroasiatic family of languages – these share a common vocabulary of terms relating to rice and rice farming, making the impression of a connection between farming and Austroasiatic unavoidable. Today the Khmer and Vietnamese languages, both Austroasiatic, are dominant in Cambodia and Vietnam, while other languages of the same family are spoken by minorities from Yunnan to Malaya and eastern India. There was an ethnic distinction between the immigrant farmers and the indigenous foragers, the skulls and teeth of the farmers showing a distinctively East Asian morphology, while the hunter-gatherers were more closely akin to modern Australian Aboriginals and Melanesians.

Very little is known about this period in Cambodia, but as an example of the very earliest stage in the Southeast Asian Neolithic we can look at Man Bac, about a hundred kilometres south of Hanoi and dating to 1800–1500 BC. The people of Man Bac lived in a high-density village community relying on herds of semi-domesticated pigs supplemented by fishing and foraging. The bones from their rubbish tips suggest that they ate a far narrower range of food than their hunter-gatherer ancestors, and their own bones

LEFT
Burial at Man Bac.

37

show that they had terrible teeth and suffered from many infectious diseases.

Those bones were found in a separate village cemetery, which is significant: it shows that the dead continued to be regarded as part of the community. One of the most touching of the burials was the skeleton of a young man born with a congenital condition that left him paralysed and bedridden by his teens. He would have been a burden to his family, unable to fish, forage or help tend the village pigs, or to drink or feed himself unaided, or clean himself of his faeces. Yet he lived to his mid-twenties, and the condition of his bones tells us that he was constantly tended. Indeed, the absence of evidence of bedsores suggests a quality of care equal to what one would expect in a good modern-age care centre.

There are two lessons to be learnt from the cripple of Man Bac. Firstly, the changeover from a nomadic to a sedentary life had made this young man's extended life possible – a nomadic band would not have been able to provide him this level of attention. Secondly, this example reveals that the village people cared for family. The village dwellers may have been sicklier than the hunters and gatherers, but when even the weakest among them could survive and potentially have children, foraging as a lifestyle was doomed.

The remains from the village cemetery show a mingling of East Asian and Australo-Melanesian remains, with the East Asian element dominating. The same is broadly true of other Neolithic sites throughout Southeast Asia, with the native Australo-Melanesian element increasing with distance from the most easily travelled river and coastal routes. The most extreme case is at the Cambodian site of Phum Snay between the Tonle Sap and the Dangrek Mountains, where Australo-Melaensians make up the majority of burials. As the people of Phum Snay were farmers, this suggests that the native Cambodian hunter-gatherers took up farming and competed on equal terms with the incoming East Asians.

Another site worth mentioning is An Son, west of Ho Chi Minh City, occupied from 2100 BC, the beginning of the Neolithic, to 1050 BC, the beginning of the Bronze Age. Pigs were present throughout the period, but it was not until around 1800–1600 BC that they became clearly domesticated. There are no remains of cattle, but there were domesticated dogs – they were a food item. Domesticated dogs and pigs were supplemented with fishing (including turtle-ing – the An Son people ate a lot of turtles), hunting and, of course, rice. Houses were built on posts, and domestic animals may have been kept under the houses, as they are in Thailand and Cambodia today. Worth noting from the point of view of the health of the population is the fact that the village was in the middle of its own refuse dump, centuries old by the end of occupation, with all that meant for rats and disease.

BRONZE AND IRON

Bronze was introduced into Southeast Asia from China in around 1000 BC. There was no large-scale migration associated with the introduction of the new technology, which seems to have followed the trade routes established during the Neolithic.

Bronze is an alloy of copper and tin, less brittle than stone and capable of being cast in many shapes. It can be tough or soft depending on how much tin it contains. Typical items from Southeast Asian assemblages include axes for clearing land and spearheads for making war, but also rings, earrings, anklets, armbands, bells and drums. Clearly bronze was a prestige product as well as a useful one, well adapted to displays of social rank in an increasingly wealthy and stratified society.

The adoption of bronze involved a quantum leap in specialization (mining, smelting and mould-making) and in trade (deposits of copper and tin are rarely found conveniently together). It also led to an acceleration in the formation of chiefdoms. The process is clearly visible in the upper valley of the Mun River, just to the north of the modern Thai-Cambodian border, where there are many villages frequently within a day's walk of each other. One of these villages, Ban Non Wat, is especially significant because it was established before bronze arrived and illustrates the social impact of the transition to metal. The Neolithic burials are typically democratic and humble – all the graves are the same, and all contain similar grave offerings. The quality and quantity of the offerings show a sharp spike as soon as bronze comes into use, and after a few generations a clear social split emerges, with poor burials continuing around the edge of the graveyard, while those in the centre are buried with metal tools and ornaments, along with dozens of finely decorated pots and thousands of shell beads imported from the coast. Presumably the individuals (families actually) buried in the centre of the graveyard held just as commanding a position over the poor in life as they did in death.

Inequality and stratification existed not only within villages but also between them. At Non Nok Tha, not far from Ban Non Wat, all the dead

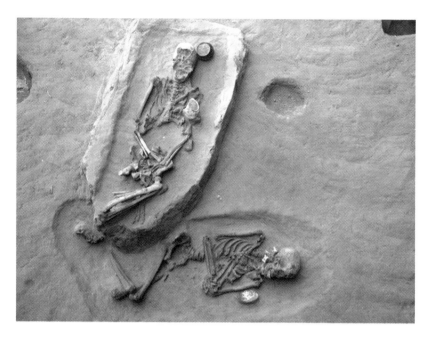

were poor, with virtually no imported beads and very few pots. The same is the case at the famous site of Ban Chiang further north, where the Southeast Asian Bronze Age was first discovered. The difference presumably reflects Ban Non Wat's good fortune in lying on a major trade route.

The most famous Bronze Age site in Cambodia is probably Samrong Sen, a shell midden on the banks of the Chinit River near Kampong

Chhnang at the north-east corner of the Tonle Sap lake. Discovered by French archaeologists in the late 19th century, it was pretty much devastated by the time Cambodian archaeologist Ly Vanna visited it in 2001:

> *The site holds at present a population of 1,237, all Cambodians. Before 1975 most of the cultural deposits of the mound were damaged due to digging for shells.* [The villagers were burning the shells to produce lime, which is chewed with betel leaves and areca nut as a mild narcotic.]
>
> *From 1975 to 1978* [the Khmer Rouge period] *the site served as a regional centre for agricultural development, and was mostly flattened by tractor. From 1978 to 1995 it became a battleground* [between Khmer Rouge and anti-KR forces], *and most of its parts were trenched either by soldiers or villagers. In the middle stands a new pagoda...*

Samrong Sen was occupied between 1749 and 1253 BC, which places it in the Bronze Age. Excavators and villagers have found bronze spearheads, axes, bracelets, a bell, and moulds and crucibles for working metal. The availability of bronze did not mean the end of stone, and the people of Samrong Sen also used polished stone adzes, gouges and chisels, from which we can infer that they were able to plane timber into planks for houses (stilt houses, because the site floods in the monsoon) and boats. Iron slag (the glassy residue left after smelting iron ore to remove the metal) has also been found, but

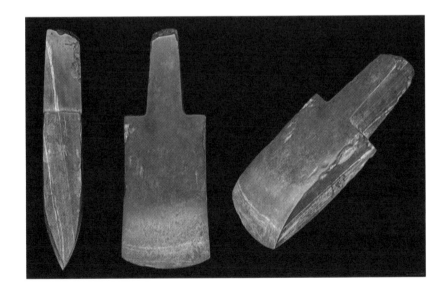

LEFT
Adzes or axes from the Bronze Age site of Samrong Sen.

due to the churning of the site over the last century it is not possible to date the Iron Age habitation.

Iron, the fourth most common element on the planet, is far easier to find than tin and copper, and unlike bronze it can be easily resharpened when blunt. It arrived in Southeast Asia in around 500 BC, and settlements on the Khorat plateau of north-east Thailand increased dramatically from around 5ha (12 acres) to more than 20ha (50 acres), implying populations of up to 2,000 people.

The Mun and Chi valleys of north-east Thailand are thickly scattered with these Iron Age settlements, which were not yet towns but can be described as super-villages. In the early Iron Age there was a wide variety of burial containers, but in the middle Iron Age the various settlements began to adopt uniform ways of burying their dead that differed from those of other communities. It is speculated that this may have been an attempt by elites to construct distinct community identities and so differentiate themselves from their neighbours. Differences between classes within settlements were shown in other ways, such as the burial of important individuals in graves filled with rice. The beginning of the Iron Age, incidentally, marks the first certain signs of domesticated water buffalo in the region, although the domestication originated in southern China considerably earlier.

The Iron Age in Cambodia is represented by Phum Snay, about 80km (50 miles) north-west of Angkor. The dates of the prehistoric settlement begin in the 5th century BC, the dawn of the Southeast Asian Iron Age, and continue through to the 3rd century AD. The site covers a very large area, and has been badly damaged by looting. The burials (type of grave, orientation of skeletons) are similar to those in Thailand from the same period, and add to the large body of evidence that the two regions should be regarded as part of a single Iron Age culture stretching north and south of the Dangrek Mountains. Some of the many graves are rich in grave goods, others are poor and some have nothing at all. The elite was buried with lapis lazuli and carnelian baubles, bronze and iron bangles, and glass beads imported from Thailand and Vietnam. One interesting group of items are the *kendi*, globular pots with a spout but no

42

handle, used for drinking and in religious rituals. Vaguely reminiscent of a coffee pot, the form probably originated in India and in time spread as far as China and Japan; it even appears as a touch of Oriental exotica in Dutch Delftware. Such items are in addition to utilitarian items such as sickles and digging implements.

In keeping with the idea that the arrival of the Iron Age in any culture means an outbreak of violence, the graves of Phum Snay contain a large number of swords and other weapons, and slightly more than 23 per cent of the dead show signs of traumatic injury, especially to the head. The proportion is far higher than from any other site in Southeast Asia.

FUNAN

The American anthropologist Robert Carniero defined the state as 'an autonomous political unit, encompassing many communities within its territory and having a centralized government with the power to collect taxes, draft men for work or war, and decree and enforce laws'. The first societies in Cambodia that might fit this definition emerged in the last half of the first millennium BC in the Mekong delta. The annual floods make for extremely fertile soil, and agriculture was probably based on flood recession, meaning that the villagers stored floodwater in artificial ponds during the wet season to be released to bunded fields in the dry season. This is a way of life and of farming that encourages, even demands, cooperation and organization, and thus leads to the emergence of chiefs and leaders.

The density of villages increased with the beginning of the Iron Age in around 500 BC, followed soon after by the first cities. Angkor Borei, near the Vietnamese border south-east of Phnom Penh, was founded in around the 4th century BC. The site is on the edge of a seasonally flooded back-swamp smaller than Tonle Sap but comparable in many ways. There were approximately 16,000ha (40,000 acres) of flood-recession rice land within a 10km (6-mile) radius of the town, and if this produced 1.5 tons of rice per hectare in ancient times (half the modern production), equating to 24,000 tons of rice per year, then this close-urban area could, hypothetically, have supported approximately 120,000 people.

The Bassac River connects Angkor Borei to the Mekong and the interior, while in the wet season an overflow connects it to the Gulf of Thailand, making it an ideal site for trade. A wall of earth and brick, 6km (4 miles)

CITIES AND CIVILIZATIONS

How do archaeologists recognize cities? To put that another way, how do they distinguish cities and towns from other settlement types? The experts differ, but there is agreement that the idea of cities is a useful one, as their complexity reflects the societies that produce them.

No single signal, such as size or the presence of writing, defines cities, but there is a range of criteria relating to their role in administration and the expression of political power, religion, economic-trade functions, and the definition and dissemination of culture. Each of these leaves distinctive traces in the archaeological record, such as palaces and temples, trade goods brought in from outside the immediate area, the existence of formal public spaces, and differences in types of dwelling and grave.

'Civilization' as a concept is even harder to pin down than cities, but one definition links it to the increasingly complex set of interactions – economic, political, military, diplomatic, social and cultural – that emerged along with urban life. The basic elements of Cambodian civilization can be traced back to earliest prehistory, but with the rise of the first cities it began to take on the distinctive traits that have continued, much changed but without catastrophic breaks, to the present day.

long and 20m (65ft) wide, was constructed around the city between the 1st and 3rd centuries AD, with multiple rebuilding and remodelling in later centuries. The wall had no guard towers, bastions or gates, which would have severely limited its military usefulness – possibly it was used for flood control and as a wet-season road above flood level.

Inside the wall archaeologists have found the brick foundations of temples, some containing statues of Indian gods, usually Vishnu. Similar finds throughout the delta date the arrival of Indian religious culture to the 5th century AD, well after the foundation of Angkor Borei and other cities. Other buildings, even palaces, were of timber, as solid masonry was reserved for the gods, a division that endured in Cambodian culture until the coming of the French.

South of Angkor Borei was a seaport known today as Oc Eo in Vietnamese and O'Keo, 'precious canal', in Khmer. It was established in the 1st century, abandoned in around AD 300, reoccupied, and finally abandoned for good in the 7th century. Archaeologists have found signs of a thriving international trading entrepot, including objects from Rome, Persia and India. More than 90 sites of the 'Oc Eo culture', as Vietnamese archaeologists term it, dating between 170 BC and AD 540, have been discovered between Oc Eo and Ho Chi Minh City, and there are more across the border in Cambodia.

In the 1930s a French official, Pierre Paris, discovered an extensive network of ancient canals in the delta (two important canals are named after him). They were apparently dug for local transport and most are just a few kilometres long, but one connecting Angkor Borei with Oc Eo is 20m (65ft) wide and 200km (125 miles) long. It was excavated or re-excavated between the 1st century BC and the 1st century AD, and the amount of labour and degree of organization involved point to the conclusion that the two cities belonged to a single kingdom commanding considerable wealth and manpower.

Funan was positioned on the trade route between India and China. The trade began around the time Angkor Borei was founded, and during the first centuries of the first millennium AD it was enriching states all around Southeast Asia. These included the city-states of Dun Sun in the isthmus connecting Thailand with Malaysia, where in the 3rd century 'east and west meet together so that daily in the market are innumerable people, precious goods and rare merchandise [and] there is nothing which is not for sale', as a Chinese history tells us. The Chinese also tell us that at this time 'the king of Funan ordered the construction of great ships', which he filled with warriors and sent to Dun Sun, with the result that 'the five kings all acknowledge themselves as vassals of Funan'. Fan Shih-man, the

ABOVE LEFT AND RIGHT
Funan-era gods – the monkey probably represents Hanuman, a figure from the Indian epic of the Ramayana, *still a central part of Cambodian culture.*

BELOW
Two kendis, spouted ewers, Oc Eo culture.

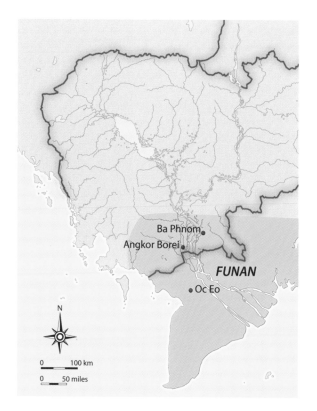

king in question, 'extended his territory five or six thousand *li*', which would have him ruling as far away as Bangladesh. From evidence such as this George Cœdès concluded that Funan was a unified state and at times a great empire, but firm evidence for this is lacking. Probably it cycled between periods of unity and disunity, but the archaeological evidence suggests that Angkor Borei was the most important city of Funan and may have been a capital in some periods of its history.

The trade that underpinned the wealth of Funan, and probably prompted its birth, was largely carried out using Southeast Asian ships. The Chinese noted that these were ubiquitous throughout the southern seas, and a Chinese dynastic history, *The History of the Liang*, notes that the ships of Funan carried up to 100 men. The remains of one ship dating from between 260 and 430 have been found in Pahang in Malaya; it apparently came from Oc Eo and was carrying rice.

Every region of Southeast Asia touched by the India-China trade adopted aspects of Indian culture, but it is clear that the process was controlled by Southeast Asians. One telling detail is that from the first inscription (found, fittingly, in Angkor Borei), the elaborate hierarchy of Cambodian ranks and titles was in Khmer, not Sanskrit, implying that the administrative structure developed in situ and was not brought from India as a complete package by colonists and conquerors. The elements of Indian culture adopted in Southeast Asia were largely those that concerned the court, such as cosmology and the high gods, writing, architecture, sculpture, and anything else that could expedite government and magnify royal prestige. Not adopted were such things as the Indian caste system, the patriarchal Indian social system and its subjugation of women, or any Indian language other than Sanskrit.

The Chinese histories are an invaluable source of evidence for this period, and the *History of the Southern Qi*, a dynasty that existed for just 23 years (AD 479–502) brings ancient Funan vividly to life:

The people of Funan are malicious and cunning. They abduct and make slaves of the inhabitants of neighbouring towns who do not pay them homage. As merchandise they have gold, silver and silks. ... The sons of great families cut brocade to make themselves sarongs, the women pass their heads [through a piece of material], *the poor cover themselves with a piece of cloth. The*[y] *make rings and bracelets of gold and plates of silver. They cut down trees to make their dwellings. The king lives in a storied pavilion. They make their city walls of wooden palisades. ... They make boats ... When the king travels he goes by elephant. Women can also go on elephants. ... The people have cock fights and pig hunts. They have no prisons. In case of dispute, they throw gold rings and eggs into boiling water; these must be pulled out. Or else they have a red-hot chain; this must be carried in the hands seven steps.*

Another dynastic history, the *History of the Liang*, adds more details:

They do not dig wells, [but] *several scores of families have a pond in common where they draw water. Their custom is to worship the sky spirits. ... When the king sits down he sits sideways, raising his right knee and letting his left knee fall to the ground. ... In times of mourning the custom is to shave off the beard and hair. There are four kinds of burial for the dead, burial by water, which consists of throwing the corpse into the river, burial by fire, which consists of reducing it to ashes, burial by earth, which consists of burying it in a pit, and burial by birds, which consists of abandoning it in the fields.*

China by this time had developed a highly sophisticated style of government, one in which foreign non-Chinese kingdoms were expected to recognize the central importance of the Chinese court by sending tribute, and in the year 539 King Rudravarman of Funan, probably residing at Angkor Borei, sent a live rhinoceros to the emperor. It was a remarkable gift, but after three more tribute missions in the next 80 years Funan disappears from the Chinese records, presumably the victim of changing trade routes as ships began taking a more direct route that avoided the delta. Funan became depopulated, and in 1818 a Vietnamese mandarin declared, quite mistakenly, that it had 'never yet been trodden by human foot'.

CHENLA

According to the Chinese annals Funan was conquered by Chenla, a former vassal kingdom located upriver, but Bhavarman, the founder of Chenla, was a grandson of the Rudravarman of Funan who sent the rhinoceros to the Emperor of China. This matters because of a story about the end of Funan and the origins of Angkor that keeps cropping up in popular histories. It holds that the last Funanese royalty fled to Java after their defeat by Chenla, laying the groundwork for an invasion of Cambodia by their descendants, who founded Angkor two centuries later. The story has no basis in history. For that matter the kingdom of Chenla has no basis in history, or not, at least, under that name, for it never appears in Cambodian inscriptions.

Modern historians treat Chenla as the region between the lower Mekong and the Tonle Sap basin in the period 550–800 AD. Like Funan, it presumably began as a collection of chiefdoms based on rice-growing villages, with the usual processes of competition in a constricted geographic area. Presumably the chiefdoms supplied Funan with the forest products in demand in the markets of India and China, and gradually transformed into states. In the second half of the 6th century, a king named Bhavavarman established himself in the valley of the Sen River, north of the Tonle Sap Lake,

BELOW

Main kingdoms of Chenla in the time of Jayavarman I (late 7th century).

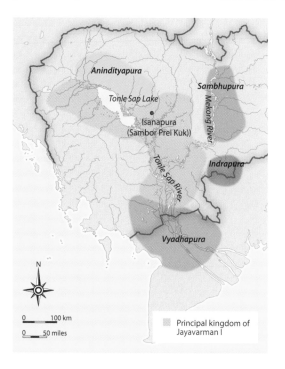

as a paramount ruler over various vassal kings. His brother and successor, Mahendravarman, also known as Chitrasena, left inscriptions recording his conquest of Sambhupura, a kingdom that controlled the Mekong from Kratie to Ratanakiri, and sent military expeditions to the Mun River in north-east Thailand. In the first half of the 7th century Mahendravarman's son, Isanavarman I, extended the kingdom still further and built himself an impressive capital called Isanapura in Kampong Thom province. Its ruins, now known as Sambor Prei Kuk, were recently given UNESCO World Heritage listing, and perhaps their most interesting feature is a series of a dozen carved faces with moustaches, long, curly hair, big eyes, thick eyebrows and pointy noses. Clearly these are not Khmers, but just who they are remains a mystery. The Chinese *History of the Sui* describes the glory of Isanavarman and his city:

> [Isanapura] *contains more than twenty thousand families. … In the middle of the city is a great hall where the king gives audiences and holds court. … Every three days the king proceeds solemnly to the audience hall and sits on a couch made of five kinds of aromatic wood and decorated with seven precious things. Above the couch there rises a pavilion hung with magnificent fabrics; the columns are of veined wood and the walls of ivory strewn with flowers of gold. … The king wears a dawn-red sash of ki-pei cotton that falls to his feet. He covers his head with a cap laden with gold and precious stones, with pendants of pearls.*

There follow further details of the king's costume, then a description of Isanavarman in formal audience:

> *Those who appear before the king touch the ground in front of them three times at the foot of the steps of the throne. If the king calls them … they kneel, holding their crossed hands on their shoulders…*

Of the ordinary inhabitants of the city the history has this to say:

> *The men are small in stature and of dark complexion, but many of the women are fair. All of them roll up their hair and wear earrings. They are lively and vigorous in temperament. … They wash every morning, clean their teeth with little pieces of poplar wood, and do not fail to read or recite their prayers… The custom of the inhabitants is to go around always armoured and armed, so that minor quarrels lead to bloody battles.*

Isanavarman died in about 637 and was followed by his son, Bhavarman II, about whom little is known. The next king, Jayavarman I, was not related to the dynasty of Bhavavarman and Isanavarman, but he was the longest reigning of all the Chenla kings and an aggressive warrior who expanded his lands to take in most of modern Cambodia. He was succeeded by his daughter, Jayadevi, who married the king of Anindityapura, a kingdom located north of the Tonle Sap Lake, and when her husband died shortly afterwards she

ABOVE
A carving at Isanapura (Sambor Prei Kuk).

ruled alone until her death in around 720. There is little inscriptional evidence available for events in the 8th century, but the temples became steadily larger and more elaborate, implying peaceful conditions and wealthy kings with control over large populations.

KINGS AND TEMPLES

Chenla was Khmer (just under half the inscriptions are in Khmer, the rest in Sanskrit), although doubtless with a much higher proportion of non-Khmer minorities than it has today, and it had a court magnificent enough to impress Chinese visitors. Its neighbour to the east was Champa (relations with Champa in later times were often hostile, but a Cham prince married a daughter of Isanavarman). To the west were the Mon-speaking Buddhist city-states of Dvaravati in the valley of the Chao Phraya River – a few Khmer princes began to establish themselves in the Mon lands in the 7th century, but it did not become part of the Khmer kingdom until the 11th century. To the north there were small kingdoms in Laos and in north-east Thailand. Chenla had relations with all these, and with China, India, Java and Sumatra.

In China the essential institution was the imperial bureaucracy, but in Chenla it was the temple. The temples were roughly analogous to medieval monasteries, controlling land and people and combining piety with wealth, but unlike European monasteries they belonged to the family that endowed them, not to any independent organization such as a religious order. They probably had their origins in the excavation and maintenance of *trapeang*, the community ponds that have been a feature of Cambodian life from ancient times to the present. The organization of labour for this was the business of chiefs called *pon*, who were heads of clans and priests serving female village ancestor spirits called *kpon*. *Pon* is by far the most common title in the inscriptions, and *pon* ranged in status from local landowners to the sons of kings. They were so numerous that the boundaries of temple lands could be described by referencing the fields and *trapeang* of neighbouring *pon*.

The temples supported the villages, but the potential output of temple lands and associated craft workshops often exceeded what was needed for self-sufficiency, and it seems that *pon* were specializing in various forms of production. Through this they could build up wealth and connections with other *pon* by trade and marriage. Canny *pon* could accumulate numerous temples and estates, and the greatest of them could support or challenge

LEFT AND OVERLEAF
Temples were the basis of the wealth and status of the Chenla aristocracy. Stone inscriptions left in these temples provide our most important source of information about this period of Cambodian history.

kings. Isanavarman described the *pon* as 'clinging vines' who depended on him for support, but in fact he relied just as much on them.

Michael Vickery, a scholar who did much to establish the current understanding of pre-Angkorian Cambodia, was the first to demonstrate that the temple inscriptions, especially in Khmer, can be used to draw an outline of Chenla's social and economic history. One representative inscription lists two-dozen record keepers, 19 'leaf sewers' (probably in charge of making plates and cups for the daily service of the gods), 17 dancers and singers (providing entertainment to the gods was an important part of daily worship), and various craftspeople, including potters, weavers and spinners. All these were of high or fairly high status, and many were women. Below them in status were the agricultural labourers. One temple had 59 field workers, 46 of them women, which seems an unbalanced ratio – perhaps the women were engaged in planting out rice seedlings, as women do today, with the shortfall of men being made up in the craft specialists. There is no mention of irrigation, or of ploughing, although there is reference to water buffalo and

the use of a yoke. Outside the temple estates we can speculate that there were ordinary free people who were humble peasants and craftspeople, just as they are today. They are referred to obliquely in the inscriptions as, for example, when the public are warned not to cause hindrance to the temple and its officials, not to steal or borrow from the temple or use its slaves, and not to seize its cattle or carts, or build houses on its land, which hints that they were doing exactly these things.

There is a great deal of argument about slaves in Chenla and Angkor. They certainly existed, but their origins and status remain unclear. Individuals captured as prisoners-of-war or on slave-raiding expeditions against the tribal people were presumably at the level of chattel slaves, and the names of the most lowly, when these were recorded, are frequently derogatory ('Dog', 'Stink'), but higher ranking slaves such as the dancers and singers could have poetic Sanskrit names ('Jasmine Flower'). Michael Vickery feels that the word used to denote this social class, *knyom*, originally meant no more than a junior member of the clan, at the beck and call of the *pon*.

Land was privately owned (tribal-era communal ownership had evidently long been overcome), and fields could be gifted or mortgaged. That which can be owned and gifted can be also be inherited, but in the early stages of Chenla's history this created a problem, for a man's possessions and titles were inherited by his sister's sons rather than his own. *Pon* were constantly searching for ways to favour their own offspring. The Indian custom, like ours, was that a man's own sons are his heirs, and early on the wealthier *pon* began insisting that inheritance should follow the way of the Indian gods. Matrilineal inheritance gradually disappeared, and with it the title *pon* and the female *kpon* goddesses, but there are still many signs of the old matrilineal society in modern Khmer culture.

Most Chenla Khmers lived in villages, but the *History of the Sui* says there were 30 towns with a population of more than 1,000 in the early 7th century. The *nagara*, at the top of the urban hierarchy, was presumably the king's town, although the town itself was given the name of its ruler (Isanapura for Isanavarman's city), and this was also the name of the kingdom. Below the *nagara* were *pura*, towns of lower nobles who carried the title 'lord of such-and-such *pura*', and below these the *grama*, a Sanskrit word equivalent to a village or district. Rulers were usually male, but there was the notable exception of Jayavarman I's daughter Jayadevi, and an inscription from Sambhupura dated 803 records the reigns of three consecutive queens – perhaps a local attempt to solve the old problem of inheritance in a matrilineal society.

The Chinese assumed that Southeast Asian kingdoms were miniature versions of their own centralized and bureaucratic empire, but a map of Southeast Asia in AD 600 would have looked similar to a map of Central Europe in 1600, a hotchpotch of territories, some large and powerful, others small and weak, some entirely inside others, some in widely separated patches, the whole united through a complex pattern of personal allegiances. Isanavarman's kingdom seems to fit this model, his authority being strongest in his core area around Kampong Thom and Prey Veng, while elsewhere local lords invoked his name in their inscriptions while making their own political decisions and appointing their own officials.

In such a system the stronger sub-rulers are always ready to set up as kings in their own right if there is a chance to do so. Jayavarman I, a member of a powerful family from Vyadhapura in the far south-east, possibly came to power due to this weakness in the system. He took vigorous steps to put an end to it, discouraging his subordinates from founding religious estates, and creating new bureaucratic posts for them with prestigious titles and emblems of office such as the coveted white parasol. The overall result was that prestige and rank now derived from the king rather than from personal wealth and position. He was also the first king to use the title *vrah kamratan an* while still living – previously reserved for dead kings and for gods (and meaning, presumably, that the dead king had joined the ancestors), it now became the Khmer equivalent of 'His Majesty'. This did not quite mean that the king was regarded as a god: Christianity sees the divine as sharply separated from the human, but outside the Abrahamic world people commonly see the two as stages of a continuum, the ancestors merging with the gods and the kings with the ancestors. It does, however, suggest that Jayavarman I had vastly raised the prestige of kingship.

3

ANGKOR
The kingdom that defined Cambodia
9th–14th centuries

One of the most enduring modern myths about Angkor is that it was lost in the jungle until Henri Mouhot revealed it to the world. In fact, the city was never lost, and there are at least 30 Khmer inscriptions at Angkor Wat dating from between 1541 and 1731.

OPPOSITE
Angkor: the stone faces of Angkor Thom.

DISCOVERIES IN ANGKOR

In the 16th century a Khmer king made Angkor his capital for a few years and completed a bas-relief inside Angkor Wat, while in 1632 a Japanese pilgrim, Ukondayu Kazufusa from Kyoto, left an inscription telling how he had celebrated Khmer New Year there. It was hardly unknown even in France: early in the 19th century a French translation of Zhou Daguan's account of his visit to Angkor in 1296/97 was published, and a French missionary named Charles-Emile Bouillevaux saw the ruins in 1850. In Mouhot's defence he never claimed to have discovered Angkor and acknowledged Bouillevaux's visit, but the posthumous publication of his *Voyage dans les royaumes de Siam, de Cambodge et de Laos*, and his romantic explorer's death far upriver in Laos, played a minor but not inconsiderable part in stimulating French colonial interest in Cambodia.

One of the most admirable qualities of the French is their commitment to scholarship and knowledge, and one of their first acts on establishing control over Indochina was to establish the École Française d'Extrême-Orient, based in Hanoi. Angkor was, understandably, an early and important part of its responsibilities. Early work was concerned with mapping the monuments, deciphering the inscriptions and putting the kings in chronological order. Once this groundwork was in place, two mid-20th-century archaeologists directed attention to the social and economic organization of the Angkorian civilization.

The first was polymath Russian aristocrat Victor Goloubew, who in the

1930s used aerial photography to reveal that Angkor's monuments were set in an extensive network of canals and reservoirs. He also saw many small surface features that had previously gone unnoticed, including mounds that had once been the sites of houses, the depressions left by ancient ponds and the bunds that marked ancient fields clustered around them. It was clear from Goloubew's work that Angkor had clearly once been far more thickly inhabited, but just how thickly remained unknown and unsuspected.

In 1979 Bernard-Philippe Groslier, former Director of the National Museum of Cambodia and head of conservation at Angkor, published an article in which he argued that the city had once possessed 'an immense system of ... main supply channels, dykes, reservoirs, field runnels, all designed to store [and] collect rainwater and redistribute it to the meticulously planned network of rice fields below'. His hypothesis was that water had

been harvested from streams running down from Phnom Kulen, the range of sandstone hills behind the Angkor plain, and collected in artificial reservoirs to be redistributed to rice fields. The largest of these reservoirs, the West Baray, is gigantic, with an area of 16km² (6mi²) and a capacity of 53 million cubic metres of water. This system, Groslier said, would have allowed Angkor to harvest two or three rice crops a year and support a population of up to two million people (today's archaeologists doubt that there were so many harvests per year and put the population in the high hundreds of thousands). This huge population provided the workforce to erect the temples and support the dance, music and literature that continues to profoundly influence the cultures of Cambodia, Laos, Thailand and Burma. It also provided the kings of Angkor with a potential army far larger than any of their rivals could muster, whether inside or outside the kingdom.

ABOVE
*The Western Baray,
the largest of Angkor's
reservoirs.*

OPPOSITE
*Mount Kulen, source of the
waters that fed the irrigation
system of Angkor.*

Groslier's hydraulic city hypothesis had many supporters but also many critics. Its crucial weakness was that it seemed impossible to link the irrigation network together. Even the barays lacked observable inlets and outlets, which they needed if they were to function as the keys of the system (they have since been found). The critics argued that the moats and artificial lakes were symbols meant to enhance the semi-divine status of ancient kings, the temples serving as earthly models of Mount Meru, the mythical mountain at the centre of the Hindu cosmos, with the barays and moats representing the world ocean surrounding it. As recently as 2001, highly respected archaeologist could write that 'there is insufficient evidence to follow Groslier in advocating a kingdom based on irrigated rice'.

RIGHT

Observations of the greater Angkor region collected by the Airborne Synthetic Aperture Radar (AIRSAR) between 2000 and 2007. The darker areas indicate water bodies. Forested areas appear much brighter.

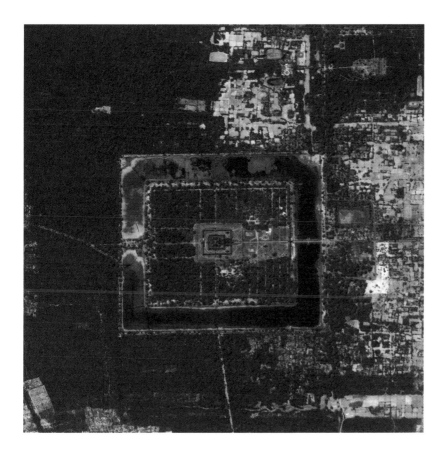

Angkor Wat. The temple complex is surrounded by a moat, representing the oceans at the edge of the universe. A stone causeway leads to the temple-mountain, home of the gods.

This view changed dramatically when archaeologists began surveying Angkor using advanced airborne radar technology that could see through the vegetation, and discovered that the system of canals at Angkor spreads further out into the countryside than even Goloubew suspected. This is not to say that the temples and moats had no symbolic significance, but the hydraulic city was real. This ancient Angkor was built of wood and bamboo. The houses, markets and workshops where hundreds of thousands of people once lived and worked are long gone, and all that remains today are the great stone temples, the homes of the gods.

Earliest Angkor was a continuation of the civilization of Chenla. Kings built unwalled cities around a central precinct containing a number of temples, each with its own moat. The king lived in a substantial wooden palace with a roof of glazed ceramic tiles, his nobles and officials had large houses next to his, and lesser mortals lived in houses of wood thatched with palm leaf. Together these buildings filled the temple precinct, which merged into a low-density suburban city of houses, gardens, paths, shrines and markets, interspersed with irrigated canals, rice fields and orchards.

Over the centuries the irrigated suburbs spread wider and wider. In the 11th and 12th centuries high-density islands began forming inside the temple precincts, as planned and regular as a modern American city – all the house mounds and house ponds inside the moat of Angkor Wat, for example, are the same size, and all the ponds are placed to the north-east of the mounds. In the 13th century the high-density urban centres began expanding into the low-density suburbs. The walls of Angkor Thom, the last major addition to Angkor and the sole walled city of the Angkorian civilization, enclosed an area of 9km² (3.5mi²), but its high-density urban centre extended over at least 35km² (13.5mi²) before merging into the low-density suburbs, which in turn occupied at least 1,000km² (386mi²). By the late 1200s, Greater Angkor formed an unbroken landscape of temples, villages, roads, dams, canals and flood embankments.

KINGSHIP AND EMPIRE

The kings of Angkor needed to extract taxes, raise armies, mobilize work-forces, dispense justice, deal with threats both external and internal, and intercede with the gods on behalf of their people. Supporting them was a large and sophisticated bureaucracy, including the *senapati* (chief of the army), tax collectors, warehouse supervisors, engineers, surveyors, architects and keepers of archives, not to mention more obscure but quite essential specialists such as court astrologers, fan bearers and pages of the royal bed-chamber.

The names and careers of some of the high officials are known to us. There was Sangrama, 'the servant with the fly-whisk', who was actually a general. There was Sri Nivasakavi, who was *hotr*, a priest skilled in incantations, to the second and third kings of Angkor, and the learned Sivasoma, tutor to the king and disciple of the Indian philosopher Shankara. It was Shankara, incidentally, who defined the key difference between Hindu and Buddhist philosophy as being that the first holds that the self exists and the second that it does not.

These officials belonged to old and noble lineages connected by blood and marriage to the royal clan. Sivasoma was the grandson of a king named Jayendradhipativarman and first cousin once removed of Jayavarman II, the founder of Angkor. Such families, of royal descent but increasingly distantly connected to the king, and with their own sources of wealth and power could, and quite often did, become sources of instability.

At a lower level were provincial officials. There were, for example, the *khlon visaya*, whose responsibilities included collecting taxes and keeping local records of land ownership. These worked through, and often were drawn from, the local nobility, yet were distinct from it in that they served the court. Lower still the districts and villages had their appointed *khlon sruk*, distinct from the village elders. There were also the *tamrvac*, who took an oath of personal loyalty to the king and combined the roles of inspectors and spies: 'If His Majesty orders us far away to obtain information on any matter we will try to learn the thing in detail ...'

Land and the population it supported was the source of wealth and power, and also the source of endless disputes. A certain Sahadeva, the rightful owner of a piece of land (or so he says), describes how this property was first obtained by his maternal great-grandfather, a man of the utmost wisdom and one who always observed the law. His inscription tells us how King Rajendravarman confirmed the ancestor's ownership of the land in question. Boundary markers were erected on it, but on Rajendravarman's death three wicked men named Pu, Hi and Ke, the last a kinsman of Sahadeva, tore down the markers. Sahadeva appealed to Rajendravarman's successor, Jayavarman V, who ordered his ministers to inquire into the matter. When they upheld Sahadeva's rights he ordered that Pu, whose hands had removed the boundary markers, should have those hands amputated, and that Hi, who had given the order, should have his lips cut off. Ke was handed over to Sahadeva along with his family, and his fate is not recorded. On Jayavarman's death Ke's family made a renewed attempt to take the disputed land, but Sahadeva appealed to Jayavarman's heir, Jayaviravaman, who ordered another inquiry. The court found again for Sahadeva, and this time the offenders were put to death. Sahadeva then erected this inscription to confirm his ownership of the land and record the justice of the king, whose word was law.

The king's charisma took concrete form in the great temples of Angkor. These expressions of the greatness of the king, growing bigger and more awe-inspiring with succeeding reigns, were political statements addressed to everyone who saw them, but especially to the great nobles. The pioneering French scholar of Southeast Asian civilizations, Paul Mus, suggested this as a way of reading the Bayon, Jayavarman VII's state temple, with its gigantic faces staring out from a forest of towers:

> *Perhaps each tower corresponded to ... a religious or administrative centre of the province ... the four faces symboliz*[ing] *the royal power spreading over the land ... signify*[ing] *that Jayavarman's royal power was as strong in the provinces as at Angkor itself.*

Beyond the city, which the king administered directly, was a circle of inner provinces ruled by princes or royally appointed governors, and beyond that a circle of tributary kingdoms where the king was acknowledged but not necessarily obeyed. Powerful kings could bend nobles and vassal kings to their wills, but weak kings could see the periphery and even the inner provinces collapse around them. If they were truly unfortunate or incompetent they could lose the core as well, and a new king would take over. Beyond the inner and outer circles were foreign kings, the most important being those of Champa, of Bagan in Burma, and of course the Emperor of China. The latter was respected as an overlord and Bagan as an equal, but the kingdoms of the Chams were most often simply enemies.

THE KINGS OF ANGKOR

Twenty-two kings reigned at Angkor between AD 800 and 1200, the period for which reasonably reliable records are available. Like the emperors of ancient Rome, theirs is a story of fratricide and civil war, sons following fathers, elder brothers following younger ones (but never the reverse), cousins following each other, all according to some principle that continues to elude discovery. Sometimes the succession was peaceful, often it was not. What seems to have mattered most was descent from significant royal women, and after that the ability to fight or negotiate one's way to the throne through a horde of equally qualified rivals.

The founder of Angkor was Jayavarman II (the regnal numbers were given by French historians reconstructing Cambodia's ancient history and no connection is implied between this king and Jayavarman I). There are two versions of his career, and it is necessary to give both. The older one begins with the conquest of Funan by King Mahendravarman of Chenla, who died in about 611. The Funanese royal family was forced to flee, and some of them, or their descendants, made their way to Java. There they were instrumental in the rise of the Sailendras, whose name, like the name of Funan, means King of the Mountain, a reference to the ancient Khmer fascination with sacred mountains. The Sailendras retained a memory of their Cambodian origins, and in the 8th century a Sailendra prince sailed a fleet up the Mekong to attack Chenla. Jayavarman, then a young prince, was taken off to Java by the invaders, but by 800 the Sailendras had grown weaker and he returned to Cambodia, where he rebelled against his alien overlords and declared his country's freedom. The climactic event took place in 802, when Jayavarman held a magic ceremony on the holy Mount Kulen to keep Kambujadesa safe from Java.

This narrative is now discredited among scholars. There are many threads of evidence showing that the transition from Funan to Chenla was gradual, not catastrophic, and marked by continuity rather than by conquest, and the career of Jayavarman II can be traced from around 770 and took place entirely within Cambodia. In any case, the only concrete source for this version is a line in an inscription from Sdok Kak Thom, just over the modern border in Thailand, saying that Jayavarman returned to Cambodia from 'Chvea'. The Sdok Kak Thom inscription, however, dates from two and a half centuries after Jayavarman's time. Much of its history is now recognized to be legendary, and scholars no longer take it seriously. Even Coedès eventually came to this conclusion, writing late in his life that '[the reigns of] Jayavarman II and his son ... make up a semi-legendary period, to which

DEVARAJA, DHAMMARAJA AND CHAKRAVARTIN

Popular histories, and some scholarly works, continue to describe the kings of Angkor as living gods on the basis of the Sanskrit term *devaraja*, meaning god-king. But this word appears only once in the entire corpus of inscriptions and seems to be a translation of the Khmer phrase *kamraten jagat ta raja* ('god of the king'). Its importance has probably been exaggerated.

Righteous kings were (and are) called *dhammaraja*. Post-Angkorian Buddhist kings had to prove their merit and their right to rule by living a righteous life and by upholding the *sangha* (the monkhood),

thus bringing peace and prosperity to the kingdom. Floods and droughts were signs not that the gods were angry, but that the king lacked merit and was therefore unworthy to rule.

Common to both Brahmanism and Buddhism is the belief that a supremely meritorious king can become a *chakravartin*, the world-conquering monarch who brings peace and prosperity to all mankind. Jayavarman II declared himself a *chakravartin* in 802, and this is conventionally taken as marking the beginning of the Angkorian kingdom.

the great religious families [of the time of the Sdok Kak Thom inscription] attached the origins of their religious functions and the landowners the origins of their rights to property'.

The version now accepted by historians, based on 8th-century inscriptions, is that Jayavarman began his career in Vyadhapura in the far south-east, and by 770 had brought the neighbouring kingdom of Bhavapura under his control. Around 780 he married into the royal family of Sambhupura (Kratie), where in 790 he left an inscription recording a battle against the Chams of Panduranga (southern Vietnam). By 800 he ruled most of northern Cambodia, including Battambang and the area of Angkor. After several changes of capital, including to the recently mapped city of Mahendraparvata on Mount Kulen, he settled in the Angkor area, where he granted estates to his followers and kinfolk. In future centuries all landed property had royal beginnings, at least in theory.

Jayavarman II died in his city of Hariharalaya (modern Roluos, about 20km/12 miles southeast of Angkor) in 834 and was succeeded by his son Jayavarman III, who ruled until 877. Jayavarman III left no inscriptions and consequently is much neglected in histories of Angkor, but preserving a kingdom for 40 years and handing it on to one's successors takes as much skill as creating one. In fact, he probably enlarged what he received from his father, as the Chams appealed to China for help against Khmer aggression during his reign.

Jayavarman III is mentioned in a number of inscriptions from later centuries in connection with stories about royal elephant hunts. No doubt all Angkorian kings hunted and captured elephants, but only Jayavarman III is remembered for it. The first of the inscriptions is a claim to a forest where the king once caught an elephant, and in the next a god directs the king to capture an elephant in a forest, which he then donates to the ancestors of those who have erected the inscription. In the third he releases a sacred elephant and donates land to an ancestor of those who have erected the inscription, then proceeds to a further hunt during which more land is donated. In the fourth story the king captures, then releases three elephants, one of which seems to be a white elephant, in a newly conquered region on the boundary between Pursat and Battambang. The elephants are then followed until they arrive at a village, which the king gifts to the ancestors of those who composed the inscription. The final inscription, as one might expect, also concerns elephants and land grants. There is an important political point hidden in the tedious details: elephants are sacred, they belong to the forest and the king, and the king alone has the power to turn forest into settled land.

The succession of Indravarman I seems not to have been peaceful: 'His sword fell on his enemies ... he was appeased only by his enemies who turned their backs in surrender or placed themselves under his protection.' Later kings take up a similar theme, describing how the land previously 'filled with parasols' – symbols of authority, their multiplicity symbolizing anarchy – was 'brought under a single parasol', or a single king. He was the first to establish what became a customary three-part pattern of royal reigns, marking the beginning with major irrigation projects, then building a temple for his ancestors, and finally a royal temple-mountain housing the Siva-linga.

Indravarman's son, Yasovarman I, coming to the throne after a fratricidal war, left the city of Hariharalaya and built Yasodharapura a short distance to the north-west. Most of Yasovarman's city has long been subsumed into later developments such as Angkor Thom, but his temple-mountain, the Bakheng, became the core of Angkor. In the early 20th century, visitors could ride an elephant to the summit (a very agile elephant – the stairs are extremely steep), and today it is a popular place for sunset viewing.

Yasovarman was followed by his sons, Harsavarman I and Isanavarman II, and they by Jayavarman IV, a son of a daughter of Indravarman married to a half-sister of Yasovarman – the bloodlines of the royal clan were becoming increasingly tangled. Some histories describe Jayavarman IV as a usurper because he was not a son of any previous king, but his claim to the throne through the female line was valid in Angkorian terms. He abandoned Yasodharapura for Koh Ker in Preah Vihear province (Koh Ker is the modern name: the ancient name was Lingapura, 'City of the Linga'), although it is likely that only the court and its functionaries moved.

Jayavarman IV was succeeded by his son, Harsavarman II, who gained the throne 'thanks to a friend and his two arms', and was followed by his uncle-cousin, Rajendravarman (944–968), who moved the capital back to Yasodharapura: 'I restored the holy city of Yasodharapura, rendered it superb and charming, erecting houses ornamented with shining gold, palaces glittering with precious stones.' His inscriptions extend over the same area as those of Yasovarman I and Jayavaramn IV, from a little beyond the modern Thai border to Phnom Penh and the upper delta in the south-east, and north and south of the Tonle Sap Lake. This area can be taken as the minimal extent of the Khmer kingdom in his time.

Rajendravarman's son, Jayavarman V (968–1001), was 10 years old when he came to the throne and reigned for more than three decades. Udayadityavarman I reigned briefly after him before the throne was seized by Jayaviravarman (1001–1006), who spent his reign fighting off rivals and was eventually supplanted by Suryavarman I.

The name of Suryavarman I (1006–1050) first crops up in eastern Cambodia during the reign of Udayadityavarman, in inscriptions from officials recognizing him as their lord without calling him king. In the following years the inscriptions come closer and closer to Angkor, until in 1006 they appear in Angkor itself. The new king claimed descent in the female line from Indravarman I, which made him a legitimate contender to the throne, but he evidently faced problems in having himself accepted and was putting down opposition as late as 1010, four years after removing Jayaviravarman. In 1011, in a sign that the country was at last pacified, he called a great assembly of *tamrvac* officials – 4,000 of them – who swore to safeguard the foundations of the country and urged the king to punish with the utmost severity any from their number who might support a rival.

Suryavarman I extended the scale and scope of the royal bureaucracy, increased the irrigated area of Greater Angkor and carried out a massive colonization of the land around the western end of the Tonle Sap Lake. He also began the transformation of Angkor from kingdom to empire, conquering the Mon kingdom of Louvo (Lopburi) in central Thailand, and the Khmer-speaking areas of north-east Thailand. His outstanding building project was the Western Baray, marked in the centre by an island with a gold statue of the reclining Vishnu from whose naval issued a fountain of water.

Across the kingdom those who had supported Suryavarman I in the recent civil war erected inscriptions recording their ancestor's illustrious origins, their connections by marriage with the royal clan and their meritorious service to kings. One tells how the loyal subject's great-grandfather had been an advisor to Jayavarman II, and how he himself, a general undefeated in battle, was given responsibility for putting down a rebel noble named Arjuna who had his stronghold in the southern provinces. He destroyed the king's enemy and was given his lands as his reward.

Suriyavarman I was succeeded by his son, Udayadityavarman II, whose brother, Harsavarman III, succeeded him in 1066, the same year that William the Conqueror invaded England.

The next king, Jayavarman VI, was a native of Mahidharapura in the Mun valley of north-east Thailand, and he made no attempt to trace his ancestry to Jayavarman II. Modern scholars therefore treat him as the founder of a new dynasty, the Mahidhara kings, but it is unlikely that the concept of a dynasty had meaning at Angkor. He was crowned in 1080 by the high-ranking priest Divakarapandita, whose long career had already taken in four kings, and the fact that he and other officials carried over into the new reign suggests that the change was not traumatic.

Jayavarman VI must have been one of the more important kings of Angkor, but practically nothing is known about him. He was followed by his elder brother, Dharanindravarman I, who was killed in about 1113 by a rebellious and apparently very athletic grand-nephew: 'Bounding onto the head of the elephant of the enemy king he killed him as Garuda [a mythical eagle] on the ledge of a mountain would kill a serpent.'

The prince was crowned as Suryavarman II, and he continued the expansionary policies of his namesake, Suryavarman I. He launched three unsuccessful expeditions against Vietnam, one with a fleet of 700 ships, placed a relative on the throne at Vijaya, the most important of the Cham kingdoms, and established diplomatic relations (or tribute relations, the two being identical in Chinese eyes) with China, the first Angkorian king to do so.

He was also a great builder, and his great monument is Angkor Wat. At 200ha (494 acres), this is probably the largest religious structure ever built. The shrine of the central tower housed a statue of Vishnu, and this in itself is notable, as kings before him had taken Siva as their state god. The bas-reliefs on its walls include fascinating scenes of life at court: we see the king seated on a low throne with his right knee raised and his left knee resting, and a

OVERLEAF
Angkor Wat was intended as the funerary temple of King Suryavarman II. Built in the first half of the 12th century, it is perhaps the largest religious structure ever.

conical crown on his head, surrounded by the parasols and fans of high rank. brahmin priests prepare for an important ceremony involving the sacred fire, and a courtier kneels to present something while kneeling courtiers look on with hands over their hearts. Elsewhere we see an elaborate procession, with retainers sounding conches and drums, and in another panel we see the king setting off for war on his elephant, surrounded by his generals on their own elephants and ranks of foot soldiers below holding lances and shields.

Suryavarman II died in about 1150, and the Chams regained their independence at about the same time. He was succeeded, probably violently, by a cousin, Dharanindravarman II, who was followed by Yasovarman II. The second Yasovarman put down a rebellion by mysterious animal-headed monsters, possibly meaning tribal peoples or a peasant rebellion (in the 1920s the inhabitants of a village where a French tax collector was murdered were declared animals by King Sisowath, and thereby expelled from the world of men). He was overthrown and killed by one of his ministers, Tribhuvanadityavarman, at an unknown date before 1166.

JAYAVARMAN VII

Tribhuvanadityavarman was succeeded, in obscure circumstances, by the most famous of all the kings of Angkor, Jayavarman VII. A great deal has

ABOVE
Devatas, minor goddesses who act as celestial doorkeepers. Their descendants, the tevodas, still serve the same function, but for humans.

been written about this king and much of it is really no more than speculation. It is said, for example, that in 1177 the Chams took Angkor in a surprise naval attack and killed Tribhuvanadityavarman, but the evidence for the attack and the date are both flimsy.

There was certainly conflict, but it was not Khmers against Chams: the battle scenes carved in the wall of the Bayon temple clearly show Chams and Khmers fighting on the same side against other bands of Chams and Khmers, and a well-known inscription by a Cham prince tells how he entered into the service of Jayavarman VII after the king's victory and helped him put down rebels. Whatever happened, it was between princes, not nations.

Jayavarman VII was a son of Dharanindravarman II, and his paternal grandfather was a brother of the mother of Suryavarman II, which meant that his royal lineage was impeccable. When Yasovarman was overthrown he was in Vijaya, the central and most powerful Cham kingdom, but what he was doing there is unknown. He hurried back to help Yasovarman but arrived too late. The Phimeanakas inscription, left by his wife, takes up the story: 'So [Jayavarman] stayed, waiting for the best moment to save the earth burdened with crime.' The moment came when the Cham king, Jaya Indravarman, invaded Cambodia and killed Tribhuvanadityavarman. Jayavarman then attacked the Chams: 'Jayavarman, having waited patiently, defeated in combat Jaya Indravarman and his ocean of warriors.'

Jayavarman came to the throne in 1182, two-thirds of the way through the 600-year history of Angkor. He must have been in his sixties, but he went on to expand the empire to its widest extent ever and to build fully half the monuments of Angkor. His legacy includes the walled and moated city of Angkor Thom to the north of Angkor Wat, and his state temple, the Bayon, at its centre. The towers of the Bayon and the gates of Angkor Thom are both decorated with the staring faces that have become an icon of Angkor and Cambodia, and the outer walls of the Bayon are decorated with bas-reliefs giving a unique glimpse of life around the year 1200. Jayavarman frequently expressed his intention to rule for the benefit of his people, and perhaps these scenes are meant to express his vision of a peaceful, prosperous Cambodia. Nobles feast in a forest while cooks grill fish and pigs and carry dishes in to their masters on their heads; a rich Chinese merchant sits with his guests while servants prepare and serve the meal; a woman gives birth; two men play chess; fishermen haul in their catch; women barter in the market and a Chinese trading junk arrives.

The royal palace was just to the north of the Bayon, with the Phimeanakas temple inside its boundary wall. The palace compound opens on the east to a raised terrace faced with carved elephants. This was probably where the king and court mounted and dismounted, and may have gathered to watch

ABOVE
Presumed portrait-head of Jayavarman VII, held in the Guimet Museum, Paris.

ABOVE

The gateway of Angkor Thom, Jayavarman VII's city at Angkor.

processions and festivals. Just to the north of this is a second terrace that may have been for royal cremations and/or judgements – it was here that a famous statue of Yama, the god of death and judgement, was found by French archaeologists in the 19th century. This is now in the central courtyard of the National Museum in Phnom Penh and is called the Leper King.

Outside the city wall are the temples of Preah Khan and Ta Prohm, erected for Jayavarman's parents and deified ancestors. They were immense, not just as buildings but as institutions: one of them, Ta Prohm, housed

LEFT
*Scenes of daily life
decorate the walls of
the Bayon temple.*

BELOW
*The major temples of
Angkor, with modern
landmarks.*

OVERLEAF
*Jungle envelops the ruins of
Ta Prohm temple at Angkor.*

12,740 people, including 18 high priests with 2,204 assistants, and 615 danc-
ing girls to serve and entertain to the gods. Some 66,265 villagers provided
rice, clothing, honey, milk, vegetables and all the other necessities of life, and
gifts from the king included silk beds, sunshades, vessels of gold and silver,
musical instruments and 165,744 wax torches. When Jayavarman came to
the throne there was already a network of highways connecting Angkor to
the far points of the empire, running in straight lines and crossing rivers on
stone bridges such as the one still to be seen from the highway on the eastern
approach to Siem Reap. Jayavarman equipped them with rest houses and
hospitals, which he saw as a central obligation of kingship.

Jayavarman was a conqueror, bringing peace to his enemies by placing
them under his benevolent rule. The Khmer stretched from the far north

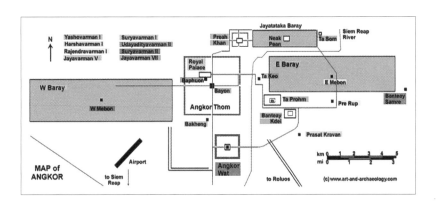

of modern Thailand to the Malay isthmus, and east to the South China Sea. The exact area covered is uncertain, but its extent in Thailand can be gauged to an extent from a list of the images Jayavarman sent to the main cities of the western half of the empire. Not all can be identified, but those that can include Lopburi, Suphanburi, Ratchaburi and Muang Singh. The last of these is near Three Pagoda Pass in the far west of Thailand, due east of modern Bangkok, and it controlled communications with the Burmese empire of Bagan. Inscriptions from Angkor suggest that quite a substantial community of Burmese was living in the city, including a very high-ranking family of priests.

The Mon lands of the west received peaceful Buddha images because the west was peaceful, but the east was the abode of the wicked Chams, and for them there was only war. Jayavarman attacked them in 1190 or perhaps even earlier, and for 20 years after 1200 all the Cham kingdoms were under Cambodian rule, or at least under the rule of Cham princes appointed by Jayavarman. In 1216, 1218 and 1220, he sent expeditions to attack Vietnam (at that time a kingdom confined to the Red River in what is now northern Vietnam), but without success.

This brings up the question of what Jayavarman would have defined as success – what was the empire building for? Michael Vickery, a Marxist, believes that he was trying to gain control of trade and the wealth that comes from it. This is no doubt true, but we should not discount less materialistic motives. A medieval Buddhist king measured his achievements in terms of how closely he represented the ideal of the *chakravartin*, the mythical Buddhist world ruler who protected and enlarged religion. This was not mere ego: it was not only the king who believed this, but his nobles, and *chakravartin*-style conquests would enhance his standing among his followers, as well as providing them with plunder and glory, and posts in the enlarged royal bureaucracy.

This also brings us to the subject of the Khmer army and how the kings of Angor fought their wars. The story is told in *The Armies of Angkor*, an enthralling study of the bas-reliefs of Angkor Wat, the Bayon and Banteay Chhmar, by Michel Jacq-Hergoualc'h of the University of Paris.

The basic battle group was a squad of foot soldiers around a single elephant, plus a few horsemen. The Cham army, also shown on the bas-reliefs, seems to have been identical. In a major battle several such units would be deployed together, the more the better. The foot soldiers are armed with bows or lances (used as thrusting weapons rather than thrown), the commanders on the elephants have swords, maces, bows, clubs and lances, and the horsemen have swords, bows and lances. All have shields and many have breastplates, or what look like quilted and padded coats, although foot soldiers frequently wear what look like thick ropes looped around their bodies – what use these were in combat is unclear. Catapults mounted on carts among the infantry and on the backs of elephants fired arrows at the enemy's elephants.

The infantry is formed up in ranks behind a wall of long, rectangular shields. The tactic, presumably, is to absorb enemy arrows before launching an attack with lances. The commander directs operations from his elephant, ready to come to grips with the enemy commander when the opposing infantry breaks, while the cavalry scout for weaknesses in his formations, carry messages between the commanders of different battle groups and, of course, attack the enemy. A forest of parasols and banners surrounds the elephants, marking the commanders and perhaps sending signals to coordinate the battle, while extras blow conch-shell trumpets and bang on gongs. These may have served to disorientate the enemy and hearten their own side, but they could also have been used to communicate between the various elephant groups.

Behind the pointy end were porters, cooks and others making up what might loosely be called the commissariat. The bas-reliefs show two men climbing a tree to hunt birds, while down below a woman carries her husband's lance, her baby, and a collection of baskets on her shoulder and head. Jacq-Hergoualc'h comments:

> [O]ne went to wage war with one's family, lance on one's shoulder, and buckler in hand, in an atmosphere of a village fair ... the heavy elephants, which they tried to protect from all sides, were above all present to impress the enemy much more than deciding the outcome of the battles, which were won or lost by the foot soldier.

The Bayon was the last grand monument built at Angkor. The temple has three ascending terraces, with a circular shrine at the centre of the highest terrace. This is now empty, but in 1933 a French archaeologist found a

Buddha seated under the hoods of a multi-headed naga serpent smashed and in pieces at the bottom of a well-like shaft in the centre of the shrine, along with an early Ayutthayan Buddha head. The absence of a dedication offering in the shaft indicates that it was dug by looters searching for gold. The presence of the Ayutthayan Buddha dates the smashing of the Buddha naga to 1430 or later, and Chinese ceramics found in another looter's pit in the temple grounds date the event to the 18th century. The Buddha was restored and is now in a pavilion on the road to the eastern gate of the city.

A forest of towers rises from the terraces of the Bayon, each featuring four gigantic faces staring out over the landscape. Popular Khmer belief holds them to be the god Brahma and links them to a legend in which a king, the founder of Angkor and of Cambodia, marries a naga princess and is warned by his father-in-law not to build four-faced towers of Brahma. The king disobeys, the naga king attacks him and is killed, and the king is cursed with leprosy.

The walls of the middle and lower terraces are covered in bas-reliefs showing battles on land and on the lake, presumably victories of Jayavarman, and scenes of daily life. These are charming, but they raise a question: what was it all about? Who was being addressed by the Bayon, and what was the message? The faces presumably express Jayavarman's Mahayana Buddhism, although exactly what they mean remains unknown. Whatever the message was it evidently offended someone, because at some point after Jayavarman's death the Buddhist iconography was destroyed and the temple was converted to Siva. The destruction is often blamed on the supposedly Saivite Jayavarman VIII, who reigned in 1270–1295, but there is very slim evidence that this king actually was a Saivite and the destruction probably happened very soon after Jayavarman VII's death.

Scattered through the temples of Jayavarman VII, including the corridors of the Bayon, are inscriptions in Khmer naming gods who seem to be posthumously deified princes, princesses and high officials. The spaces they mark were reserved for cult statues called *kamraten jagat*, meaning 'lord of the world', or 'lord of mankind'. These might be comparable to the *neak ta*, the guardians and spirit owners of places, and some are identified as the *preah rupa*, 'sacred image', of the dead person. The idea seems to be that the dead have become protective spirits in the afterlife, and are somehow absorbed into, rather than being merely represented by, their statues. In one sense, then, the Bayon was a temple built to house all the gods of the empire, whether Indian or Khmer, and it is thus a kind of error to call the Bayon a Buddhist temple (although it is), or to call Jayavarman VII a Buddhist king (although he was).

LATE ANGKOR

Jayavarman VII's empire began breaking up on his death. Champa was abandoned in 1220, Sukhothai, the north-westernmost possession of the empire, was lost in 1238, and by the end of the century the Siamese had occupied the entire Chao Phraya valley and the upper portion of the modern Thai isthmus. The losses do not seem to have bothered the kings at Angkor, who made no effort to regain the territories, or to have harmed the city: when the Chinese visitor Zhou Daguan visited Angkor in 1296 he reported that war with the Siamese had devastated the countryside, but his description of the city itself gives the impression that it was thriving.

Angkor continued to exist for at least another two centuries after Jayavarman VII, but temple building in newly quarried stone practically ceases, as do stone inscriptions. As a result the number, names and religious affiliations of the kings are uncertain – five are known in the century and a quarter after 1200, but there could well have been some who simply fell out of the record. Of those whose names are recorded, Indravarman II (c. 1220–1270) was apparently a Mahayana Buddhist, Jayavarman VIII (1270–1296) has been identified by some as a Saivite, by others as a Buddhist, and Indravarman III (1296–1308) seems to have been a Theravada Buddhist.

After Indravarman III we know of Indrajayavarman (1308–1327), and Jayavarmadeva-paramesvara, whose unwieldy name can be deconstructed as Jayavarman plus deva, meaning 'god', plus a posthumous title, making it convenient to refer to him as Jayavarman IX. He came to the throne in 1327, and is probably the king mentioned in the Lao chronicles as having married his daughter to 16-year-old Fa Ngum, the exiled Lao prince who later established the first unified Lao kingdom. If this is correct it extends Jayavarman IX's reign to around the middle of the 14th century, as Fa Ngum was born in 1316 and the founding of Lan Xang is reliably dated to 1353. Thai and Cambodian chronicles give the names and adventures of further kings to Ponhea Yat, the supposed last king of Angkor, often with considerable and very colourful detail, but they are not to be trusted.

OVERLEAF
All-seeing eyes gaze out from the towers of the Bayon temple.

ZHOU DAGUAN'S ANGKOR

Zhou Daguan's name has been mentioned several times already. He was a Chinese official who spent 11 months in Angkor in 1296/97 as a member of a diplomatic mission. He was possibly its secretary, as he seems to have taken copious notes. On his return home he wrote an account of his stay titled *A Record of Cambodia*, and as he informed his readers, 'although I could not get to know the land, customs, and affairs of state of Cambodia in every particular, I could see enough to get a general sense of them'.

The country, he begins, is called Chenla by the Chinese but Ganbozhi (Kambuja) by its inhabitants. Kambuja is rich, gold is everywhere. The city gates are decorated with gold Buddha heads, inside there are gold towers and gold bridges guarded by gold lions, officials go about their business in gold palanquins shaded by gold-handled parasols, and the wealthy classes eat from dishes of gold and silver. 'I suppose all this explains why from the beginning there have been merchant seamen who speak glowingly about rich and noble Cambodia.'

All the luxuries Zhou saw, the fine silk, pewterware, umbrellas, quality paper, iron pots, fine-tooth combs and much more, came from China (or so he says, but cotton cloth would have come from Indonesia and India). In return Cambodia offered 'precious birds and wonderful animals too numerous to count', rhino horn, ivory, kingfisher feathers, which were in great demand in China for embroidering into iridescent robes, and beeswax. The beeswax seems to have been particularly significant given the amount of detail Zhou gives: 'Each junk carries two or three thousand honeycombs ... and each large comb weighs between 40 and 45 pounds', which equates to 75–76 metric tons per junk.

Indravarman III had only recently come to the throne, and in the usual way. He had been a high military commander under his predecessor, Jayavarman VIII, probably a royal relative, and was married to the king's daughter. On Jayavarman VIII's death Indravarman's wife procured the sacred gold sword of royalty, and with this in his possession Indravarman was accepted as king ('accepted' presumably means accepted by the army, which he commanded, and the nobles, of whom he was one). We can legitimately suspect that there must have been more to it than taking possession of the sacred sword, but it clearly occupied a key place in the royal and national ethos, and Indravarman always carried it when in public. The king's son, who might have been the rightful heir, was imprisoned, where he still languished at the time of Zhou's visit.

Zhou gives a long description of a royal procession to illustrate the splendour of the barbarian king. First came the royal ministers and high court officials and members of the royal family, riding on elephants and surrounded by red parasols 'too many to number'. They were followed by the royal wives and concubines in palanquins and carts with gold filigree parasols, and the king's all-female bodyguard with lances and shields, then more women with candles and offerings, until at last the king himself appeared, mounted on an elephant with gold-sheathed tusks, gold sword in hand, surrounded by guards, elephants and white parasols, with banners, drums and musicians bringing up the rear. The spectacle was intended to impress, and it did: 'They know what it is to have a king.'

This was a highly hierarchical society, and every degree of rank was regulated and signalled by outward display. The various ranks of royal officials were distinguished by the decoration permitted for their palanquin poles and parasol handles, and by the patterns on the cloths with which they wrapped their lower bodies, from a full floral pattern for the king, down to two flowers for the most junior. Even the houses were regulated, from the sizes of the rooms to the material, tiles or thatch, permitted for the roof. Common people would never dare ape the lifestyles of their social betters,

LEFT
A king of Angkor carried in procession on a palanquin, surrounded by umbrellas and fans.

even if they could afford it, and nobles would not dare dress or act as kings.

Officials were drawn from the aristocracy. To confirm and strengthen the family basis of the relationship between them and the king it was the custom among the elite to give a daughter for the royal harem. The king, says Zhou, had thousands of these concubines. The institution survived into the 19th and early 20th centuries to scandalize the French, who failed to grasp that its purpose was essentially political, and far from trivial.

Zhou implies the presence of quite a large community of Chinese in Angkor, and it would not be unreasonable to suppose that there were similar communities in provincial towns. They shared in the wealthy lifestyle of the elite. Ordinary people lived humbler lives, but the picture Zhou gives is of a comfortable life for all – except the slaves. According to Zhou most people kept a hundred or so slaves, although some had only a few dozen. They were taken from among the savages who lived in the forests and mountains, and lived under the stilts of their masters' houses. If required to enter the house they had to kneel, join their hands respectfully and bow to the floor. Their children also became slaves, to be disposed of at the pleasure of their owner. A strong young slave could be purchased for 100 pieces of cloth, an old and weak one for 30 or 40. Slaves were caned if they misbehaved, and tattooed and shackled if they ran away.

There are some problems with Zhou's picture of slavery at Angkor. One wonders how a hundred slaves would fit under one house, or what practical use so many would be. Then there is the question of security – Zhou does not give the impression that Angkorians(one-hundredth of the total population if we take him at face value) lived in fear of a slave uprising. He does let slip quite casually that there was a night curfew, but this might have been a more general security measure.

Zhou gives a glimpse of the savages in the mountains, 'mov[ing] from place to place … carrying a clay pot on their head'. They hunted with bows and arrows, cooked and ate their kill immediately, and moved on. 'By nature they are very ferocious … and within their own groups they frequently kill one another'.

The vast bulk of the Khmer people lived lives somewhere between those of the miserable under-house slaves and the palanquined elite, but very little is known about them. They cleared land and farmed, built temples and roads, maintained hydraulic infrastructure and fought in the armies. In the city of Greater Angkor they seem to have lived comfortably – Zhou does not mention beggars – but it is unclear how much control they had over their lives. Temple inscriptions list them as *knyom*, which today is the first-person pronoun 'I', but seems then to have been closer to a social classification. They could be bought, sold and gifted, but had some freedom of movement. Their religion was probably more native Khmer than Indian, and they were probably excluded from the Sanskritic culture of the elite – a factor that may have facilitated the rapid uptake of Theravada Buddhism.

Everyone washed several times a day and perfumed themselves with sandalwood and musk (presumably the slaves were not included in Zhou's 'everyone'). Everyone, even the ladies of the court and the king himself, went bare-breasted and barefooted, adorned with rings on their fingers and toes, and bangles on their wrists and ankles. This was the cultivation of the body as ornament, universal throughout Southeast Asia until quite modern times.

Women ran the markets, and women in Cambodia and throughout Southeast Asia have always had a higher status than they enjoyed in China, India or the Muslim world. This higher status should not be interpreted as freedom per se – as the institution of the harem demonstrates, women were still the property of their families. As in the days of Chenla, trade was carried out using measured quantities of rice and cloth, with larger transactions in gold and silver. The step to regulating these by turning ingots into coins seems so simple and obvious that one can only wonder as to why it was never taken – the answer presumably lies in the way both society and the economy were organized around the temple estates, from which produce could be allocated directly.

Angkor was cosmopolitan. Chinese merchants were settling down and marrying Khmer wives. This was apparently a fairly recent development – Zhou notes that the Chinese had formerly been treated with the greatest respect, but familiarity was breeding contempt and the wily Khmers were increasingly taking advantage of the innocence of their visitors to cheat them. Zhou also notes the increasing numbers of Siamese, who were introducing the Khmer to silk and sewing, and from inscriptions we learn about apparently notable numbers of Chams, 'Yuvana' (Vietnamese from Dai Viet in the Red River valley of far northern Vietnam), Pukom (Burmese from Bagan), and Rban, who have not been identified.

Zhou offers us history's first glimpse of Southeast Asian ladyboys.

ABOVE

A naval battle, possibly on Tonle Sap Lake: Chams to the left, Khmers to the right, a crocodile in the middle.

Catamites, he says, go around the markets in groups every day, 'solicit[ing] the attention of the Chinese in return for generous gifts ... it is shameful and wicked'. Perhaps so, but in today's Siem Reap and Pattaya the Chinese are among the most appreciative fans of the ladyboy cabarets. The people, he says, regarded 'a dissolute life' as 'neither shameful or odd'. 'I have often heard' (from resident Chinese?) 'that the women are lascivious and promiscuous, [although they] age quickly'. One can only wonder, for in the 19th and 20th centuries the French regarded the Khmer as highly moral, and the infamous Phnom Penh brothels of the 1990s were staffed by Vietnamese rather than Cambodian girls.

Zhou does not tell us what happened in the case of a commercial dispute between Chinese and Khmers, but it might have gone straight to the king, who was the source of all justice. Those who wished to access this justice could prepare a petition, or have one made for them, writing in chalk on a sheet of leather dyed black. The king appeared daily in the palace, in suitable splendour, to hear the petitions and deliver necessary guidance to his ministers. If more were needed there were trials by ordeal, just as earlier Chinese visitors had witnessed in Funan, involving plunging hands into boiling oil or sitting in two towers without food or water until one party gave up, 'such is the spiritual power of the local gods' (the towers can still be seen opposite the Terrace of the Leper King).

'There are never any whippings or floggings as punishment [for crimes], only fines', says Zhou, and then lists a set of punishments that sound far from

OPPOSITE BELOW
Celestial beings guard Angkor Wat, mirroring the women of the royal court that Zhou Daguan noted surrounded Khmer kings in their palaces.

BELOW
A king hunts deer from a chariot, while on the right are lions. Given the absence of lions from Cambodia, the scene must be from mythology rather than daily life.

enlightened, including burial alive at the West Gate and amputation of fingers, toes and noses (the unfortunate prince whose claim to the throne was thwarted by Indravarman III had had his toes amputated before his imprisonment). There was clearly nothing resembling a police force: a citizen who found a dead body outside his door would drag it to wasteland outside the city, because there would be no inquest or official investigation.

Zhou distinguishes three types of holy men, 'learned men called *banjie* ... Buddhist monks are called *zhugu* ... [and] followers of the Dao are called *basiwei*'. By *banjie* Zhou seems to mean the Sanskrit word *pandita*, meaning a scholar of Sanskrit literature. The scholarship presupposes a privileged childhood and a youth of leisure, and presumably all the holy men came from elite brahmin families. Some of the literature was religious but much was practical, and evidence from inscriptions shows that pundits could occupy very high positions in the royal administration.

Zhugu seemed to be Theravadin monks. They shaved their heads and dressed in yellow robes with one shoulder bare, ate one meal a day and chanted scriptures from palm-leaf books. Zhou does not say so, but their books and chants would have been in Pali instead of Sanskrit. Kings sought their advice, and like the pundits they were entitled to parasols and palanquins.

The *basiwei* were apparently ascetics dedicated to Siva. They never ate the food of others, and they did not allow others to see them eat (in other words, they observed Hindu food taboos). They were fewer than the Buddhists, and their temples were smaller. Zhou makes no mention of any interaction with kings.

Angkor's army, according to Zhou, was a rabble. The soldiers were naked and barefooted, armed only with lances and shields, and had no bows, armour or helmets, let alone trebuchets. No doubt they were brave– the French considered the Khmer the bravest of all their Indochinese troops – but they were badly led. 'When the Siamese attacked all the ordinary people were ordered out to do battle, often with no good strategy or preparation.' Zhou's army is so different from that on the walls of Angkor Wat and the Bayon that one wonders whether we are talking about the same country. If the two can be reconciled, if the reliefs of Angkor Wat represent more than royal propaganda, perhaps we need to remember that 100 years separate Zhou from Jayavarman VII, and 150 from Suryavarman II, and that both were strong kings.

THERAVADA

Theravada was one of several schools that formed among the followers of the Buddha after his death in the 5th century BC. In the 3rd century BC it found royal patronage in Sri Lanka, and from there it spread to the Mon city-states of southern Burma and southern Thailand, where again it enjoyed support at the highest levels of society. The Chinese writers tell us that Buddhism was well established in Funan by the late 5th century, when the monk Nagasena was sent as an envoy to the Imperial court, but Nagasena told his hosts that the main religion was the worship of Siva (he would have meant the religion patronized by kings, since village religion was probably quite a different matter, as it is today). Another noteworthy monk was the learned Paramartha, a native of Ujjain in India who spent some years in Funan before King Rudravarman sent him to China with a recommendation as the leading scholar in his kingdom. It is impossible to be sure just what schools of Buddhism these and other monks belonged to, but it is reasonable to assume that both Mahayana and Theravada were represented, and that they had at least some degree of royal support.

In the late 7th century a Chinese pilgrim, reporting what others had told him, said that the people of Chenla had venerated many gods until a 'wicked king' had totally exterminated Buddhism in his realm. The time would fit Bhavavarman II, and the inscriptions bear out the minor place of

LEFT
Buddhism of the Theravada school became the religion of the Khmer people during the late Angkor period. The details of its spread remain unknown.

Buddhism in Chenla: of over 90 inscriptions mentioning Indian gods, more than half reference Siva, 14 Vishnu, eight Harihara (a combined form of Vishnu and Siva), and seven are Buddhist.

Buddhist images become quite common in the late 10th century, and in the 11th and 12th centuries the cults of Siva and Buddha increasingly shared in the common attraction of magical tantrism, culminating in Jayavarman VII's patronage of a tantric form of Mahayana. Theravada was also gaining support in royal circles, and the Burmese *Glass Palace Chronicle* tells us that in 1180 a son of Jayavarman visited Sri Lanka to be ordained into the sangha, and that a little earlier a Sri Lankan princess was shipwrecked in Burma while on her way to Cambodia, perhaps to marry a prince. Contact between Angkor and Sri Lanka was intense enough for a district of the Sri Lankan capital to be called Cambodia-Gate (Kambojavasala).

A century later, Zhou Daguan reported that Indravarman III wore a gold crown 'like the crown worn by the Holder of the Diamond', a tantric Buddhist divinity, while simultaneously patronizing Theravada monks and participating in what sounds very like a Theravada ceremonial washing of a gold Buddha image. The king later abdicated to take up the life of a meditating forest monk, and his successor, Indrajayavarman, donated a village to a senior abbot plus four more villages, with their slaves, to support the monastery. In the mid-1300s, Jayavarman IX seems to have been an exemplary royal patron of Theravada, sending monks and sacred texts to his son-in-law, Fa Ngum, so that the Way could be established in Laos.

It is clear that Theravada was advancing rapidly among both the elite and commoners, but just why is unclear. Possibly the extension of the empire into central Thailand, with its Theravadist Mon population, had something to do with it, and Zhou mentions the large number of Siamese in Angkor. He may have failed to discriminate between Mon and Siamese, and indeed the Mon and Siamese were merging to such an extent that no discrimination may have been possible, but *zhugu* seems to be Zhou's attempt to express *chao khun*, the Thai honorific for a Theravadin monk.

Cambodian Theravada developed Cambodian characteristics, and the resulting religion, one of the prime defining features of modern Khmer identity, became dizzyingly eclectic. Siva became a *neak ta*, Vishnu became the protector of kings, and Indra, the king of the gods, shares space in Buddhist prayer halls with a rich array of mythological figures. Brahmin astrologers still remained in the palace to advise kings on propitious dates, and tantric magic was taken up by skilled practitioners who were often also monks, always in the service of *dharma*. Cambodian monks took part in the Buddhist Council held in Chiang Mai in 1477, and travelled to Laos and Sri Lanka to sit at the feet of teachers; in the 19th century a great Buddhist reform movement, the Theravadin equivalent of the Reformation, spread from Thailand to Cambodia under royal patronage.

The kings became the guardians of religion, instituting a hierarchy of monks with ranks, rules and self-government, all under the king's aegis. Ostensibly this was to ensure that ordination and all that flowed from it was in keeping with the standards laid down in Sri Lanka, but the political result was that the Sangha became, and has remained, subservient to the king.

The institution of the village monastery spread literacy to the commoners. As Zhou records, every boy spent a little time as a novice, and as part of his monastic education he learnt to read and write. Cultural cohesion was spread with literacy, and with it an idea of Khmer-ness expressed in king, language and religion.

AFTER ANGKOR

Why, after six centuries, did the kings abandon Angkor in the early 15th century? One popular explanation is that the wars and building programmes of Jayavarman VII exhausted the country, but his reign ended 250 years earlier and causes should be closer to their results. Another explanation is that Theravada, being pacifist and world renouncing by nature, undermined the will to maintain the empire, but the Theravada of the Siamese and Burmese did not prevent them from waging very aggressive wars. A parallel argument is that Buddhism is democratic (anyone can be a monk), and that this destroyed the hierarchic world of classical Angkor, but as the Khmer Rouge pointed out, Buddhism excuses privilege and inequality as the working out of karma and is therefore profoundly undemocratic.

The word 'collapse' is often mentioned in connection with the end of Angkor, but the idea of a collapse is problematic. The beginning of the end is often placed in the early 13th century, largely because the expansion of the Siamese into the western parts of the empire dates from then, but the kingdom visited by Zhou Daguan at the end of the century was holding its own quite ably. This seems to have remained the case well into the 14th century, and as we will see in the next chapter, Cambodia continued to be a power to be reckoned with well after the kings moved their courts to the junction of the Tonle Sap and Mekong Rivers. Nevertheless, the population of Angkor reached its peak in the 12th and 13th centuries, then declined, and this fact demands an explanation. The Greater Angkor Project, which has been carried out since the 1990s by a joint French, Australian and Cambodian team, has been investigation this question (and others), and the evidence is still forthcoming.

The accepted picture for most of the 20th century was that the end of Angkor was sudden and even cataclysmic. French archaeologist Bernard-Philippe Groslier was working within this framework when he argued that centuries of expansion pushed the city beyond its capacity: as the irrigation system grew larger and larger it became more and more complex, and sheer complexity made it increasingly vulnerable to sudden catastrophic failure. For example, the Siem Reap River channel today is eroded 5–8m (16–26ft) below original ground level, and a major canal in the south of Angkor is entirely filled with cross-bedded sands, the result of a single massive flood. A succession of events like this over a short period could have overwhelmed the system.

Behind these weather events lies long-term climate change. The Angkor plain receives 90 per cent of its rain between May and October, and for the rest of the year it is as dry as the African savannah. Most of Cambodia shares the same climate and has to cope with the same annual drought, but Angkor was blessed with an accident of geography in the form of the Kulen hills. These captured the monsoon rain like a gigantic sandstone sponge and released it slowly over the dry season, allowing Greater Angkor to harvest water in increasingly complex irrigation works. Quite possibly it was this feature that first attracted Jayavarman II when he established the capital here in about the year 800.

Jayavarman's successors turned out to be the beneficiaries of a singular stroke of luck. The monsoons are driven by the Intertropical Convergence Zone (ICZ), and in about 900 the ICZ shifted northwards (the evidence for this comes from tree-ring analysis, which records a succession of good seasons beginning at this time). This meant that the rains became more reliable throughout Southeast Asia and harvests more dependable, and at Angkor the irrigation network expanded into previously marginal land. The

population increased, allowing kings to increase taxes, carry out massive construction projects such as temples and irrigation works, and raise larger and larger armies to raid and conquer their neighbours. This was the foundation for Angkor's steadily increasing growth and prosperity over the four and a half centuries from its foundation.

The luck ran out in the mid-1300s. The cause again was the ICZ, which now shifted south. For three decades from 1362 to 1392 the monsoons started later, brought less rain and finished earlier. Decades of drought would have been bad enough, but the southwards shift of the ICZ was unstable, and these years were followed by years of unusually strong monsoons. Between the mid-1390s and mid-1410s, heavy storms brought flash floods that overwhelmed the delicate hydraulic machinery, cutting the deep channel of the Siem Reap River and wrecking canals and embankments.

Between 1415 and 1440, the ICZ resumed its southerly shift, bringing more droughts, and at some point in these decades – the traditional date is 1431 or 1432 – the kings abandoned Angkor.

ABOVE
Monsoon clouds over rice fields. Climate change bringing increasingly frequent droughts and intense storms played a major role in the end of Angkor.

4

THE DAWN OF THE MODERN
Between Angkor and the French
15th–19th centuries

Trade between China, India, the Middle East and Europe began at the same time that states first arose, but the 15th century saw the beginning of a massive expansion in trade that continued almost without remission into the age of European colonialism. In order to understand what was happening to and in Cambodia in this long span of more than 400 years, it is necessary to look at the wider picture, as well as developments in Cambodia.

OPPOSITE
*Stupa of Ponhea Yat, Wat
Phnom, Phnom Penh.*

SOUTHEAST ASIA AND THE AGE OF COMMERCE

What sparked the great 15th-century expansion of trade was the state-sponsored treasure fleets of Admiral Zheng He on behalf of Yongle Emperor, the third emperor of the Ming dynasty. The first fleet, made up of 317 ships carrying 28,000 sailors, set off in July 1405 'bearing imperial letters to the countries of the Western Ocean and with gifts to their kings of gold brocade, patterned silks, and colored silk gauze, according to their status'. It called at Champa, Java, Malacca and Semudra, the last an important trading city on

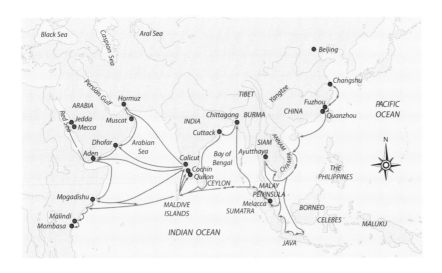

LEFT
*Between 1405 and 1433
Admiral Zheng He led seven
expeditions as far afield
as the coast of Africa. The
Chinese expansion ended
abruptly, but the prospect
of sharing in it may have
been a significant factor in
the relocation of the Khmer
capital from Angkor to the
Phnom Penh region.*

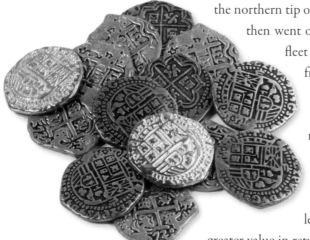

the northern tip of Sumatra, across the Bay of Bengal at Sri Lanka, then went on to southern India for a four-month stay. The fleet arrived back in China in 1407, bringing envoys from foreign kings who paid their respects to the emperor before being sent home with costly gifts.

There were seven such treasure fleets, each more impressive than the last. They represented the culmination of the Chinese tribute system by which foreign rulers sent gifts and made submission to the Chinese court, which then legitimized their rule and sent goods of equal or greater value in return. In Southeast Asia the beneficiaries included Ayutthaya in the Gulf of Thailand, Malacca and Pasai in the Straits of Malacca, Brunei in Borneo, Manila in the Philippines (already an important trading port), and Gresik and Demak in Java. Champa was visited on every voyage, but Angkor, far upriver and off the maritime highways, was never called at.

ABOVE AND BELOW
Spanish reals and doubloons; Cambodian coins of the early modern era.

After 1433 the treasure fleets ended, but private traders stepped into the gap. In this they were assisted by large Chinese expatriate communities in the ports of the region, many of them deserters from Zheng He's fleets, others refugees from the Ming wars on their internal enemies. In the 1500s, non-Chinese merchants started arriving, first the Portuguese and Spanish, later the Dutch and Japanese. In the early decades they sailed directly to the southern ports of China, but in the mid-1500s the Ming government began licensing private traders, and thereafter the foreigners did their China trade through the Chinese expatriate communities in Southeast Asia.

The expanding private trade created an immense demand for silver, and in the course of the 16th century world silver production increased ninefold to 380 tons per year. A huge amount of this ended up in Southeast Asia, the majority from Japan (130 tons each year), with smaller but respectable amounts from Spanish America via Manila (23 tons a year, around a third of the annual output of the American silver mines), and from the Dutch and English (at least 20 tons a year). Southeast Asian states like Cambodia and Siam began producing their own silver coins in the early 16th century, but the Spanish *real*, from which comes the name of the modern Cambodian *riel*, was the preferred currency of the entire region.

THE GUNPOWDER KINGDOMS

The era of internationalized trade coincided with new forms of warfare based on gunpowder. The technology was originally Chinese, and the first step, in the 10th century, was to fill a bamboo tube with powder, tie it to a spear, light a fuse and throw it at the enemy. This was far from as comical as it might sound, as the exploding bamboo produced sharp splinters that could maim and kill. Eventually bamboo was replaced with reusable metal tubes filled with shrapnel, and the first cannon was born. Chinese cannon became highly sophisticated, with multi-barrelled weapons capable of keeping up a continuous rapid fire, stacks of up to nine barrels fired simultaneously and capable of throwing a considerable weight of stone or metal, and even an early machine gun in the form of a container with 100 or more lead balls that could be sprayed out rapidly. In the mid-15th century defectors and smugglers transferred the technology to the Vietnamese and others along China's southern border, and soon locally produced cannon were to be found throughout the mainland.

China's military technology stagnated after the mid-15th century, but gunpowder had reached Europe, where a steep trajectory of constant innovation was just beginning. When the Portuguese arrived in Asia in the last decades of the 15th century, it was with weapons more advanced than any available to their opponents, combined with a long-term plan to dominate the East. In 1511 they captured Malacca, demonstrating the superiority of their breech-loading artillery and steel body armour in the process, and soon every ruler in Southeast Asia

ABOVE
Vasco da Gama, who in 1488 rounded the Cape of Good Hope and opened the Indian Ocean and Asia to direct European shipping. The Portuguese and Spanish established themselves in Southeast Asia in the 16th century, the Dutch in the 17th and 18th, and the British and French in the 19th.

LEFT
Chinese cannon, 15th century.

99

had his Portuguese military advisors, Portuguese artillery and Portuguese arquebuses (an early small arm, highly effective at short range).

The pattern continued through the following centuries, with the Europeans always having the latest innovations in military technology, and the richest and savviest Southeast Asian kings always keen to hire them as advisors and mercenaries. The result was an outbreak of warfare and empire building. Tabinshwehti and his successor, Bayinnaung, built an empire in Burma; in Java the Muslim port-cities of the north coast absorbed the Hindu/Buddhist kingdoms of the interior, and the kings of Ayutthaya consolidated their control over the other Thai principalities of what is today Thailand.

The actual business of making war was a curious mix that saw elephants fighting alongside artillery. Take, for example, Nguyen Anh, a military leader of genius who dominated events in Vietnam and eastern Cambodia in the closing decades of the 18th century because of his close bonds with French mercenaries. His army of 114,000 men included 16 elephant battalions with 200 animals and 8,000 men, 30 artillery battalions with 15,000 men, 42,000 infantry equipped with matchlocks and sabres, and trained in traditional warfare, 30,000 infantry trained in the European manner, 12,000 guards trained in European tactics and 24 squadrons of buffalo cavalry. His navy was equally impressive, and easily dominated the inland waterways of Cambodia as far as Phnom Penh.

THE GODS ABANDON ANGKOR

Sources are almost totally lacking for Cambodia's 15th century. The stone inscriptions have ended, and the Cambodian Royal Chronicles are largely fictional until they reach the mid-16th century. Nevertheless, it is to the chronicles that we owe the account of how Ponhea Yat, the last king of Angkor, shifted his capital to Phnom Penh after a devastating Siamese invasion in or around 1432 (different versions of the chronicles give different dates). The capture of Angkor by the Thais is probably true history, but a fragmentary Ayutthayan chronicle discovered in 1971 gives an intriguing alternative picture of the aftermath.

The story opens in 1441, 10 years after the Ayutthayan conquest of Angkor, and Prince Nakon In, the son of the king of Ayutthaya, is governing the city on behalf of his father (this contradicts the Cambodian chronicle, which says the Siamese occupation lasted only a year). Ponhea Yat appears, not as the last king of Angkor but as the son of a former king of Ayutthaya who was overthrown by Nakon In's father and sent to govern Chaturmukh, which is Phnom Penh. As the fragment opens he is making preparations for a revolt against Nakhon In. The events that follow are missing, and the next date is 1443. The revolt fails, and Ponhea Yat is captured. Things look bad, but Nakhon In falls ill, then very ill, then dies. Yat escapes. He begins rallying the Chong and Pear, who are tribal peoples of the Cambodian-Thai border (or rather, the area where the border would be several centuries later), and at this point the fragment ends.

The fragment shows the conflict between Ponhea Yat and Nakhon In not as one between Khmers and Siamese, but between competing factions of Ayutthayan royalty. This would not mean that Ponhea Yat was not also a Khmer: the consensus of scholars is that Ayutthaya grew gradually out of a mixed Khmer-Mon-Siamese background, and both sides may have regarded Angkor as the ancient home of their ancestors.

The stress here should be on 'ancient'. By the 15th century the Southeast Asian world had changed radically from the days of Jayavarman VII and even from those of Zhou Daguan. Wealth at Angkor had been represented by the control of land and people, but now it came from tapping into international maritime trade. In 1431, Zheng He's voyages were current events, and the kings of Angkor would have no reason to suspect that they were about to end. They were being excluded from the new Chinese-sourced wealth, and

CAMBODIAN CHRONICLES

The Cambodian chronicles are represented in two major traditions, with marked differences between them. The Nong chronicle covers the period 1414–1800, and Version II covers 1346 to the mid-15th century, with a separate fragment covering 1570–1628. Both were written at the Cambodian court in the late 18th to early 19th centuries, with the aim of showing that the King of Cambodia had always been dependent on his patron, the King of Siam.

The chronicles were probably based on a now-lost 16th-century chronicle of Longvek, and the authors had no reliable knowledge of events before

then. The supposed Angorian king Nippean Bat was invented by taking a title of Ang Chan I, the first of the Longvek kings, and the narrative between Nippean Bat and Ang Chan was then filled in with the events of the 16th century, or by copying the Ayutthayan chronicles almost word for word, or from folklore. Some genuine information is preserved, including the Siamese occupation of Angkor in the early 15th century (confirmed by archaeology) and the existence of the early 15th-century king Ponhea Yat, but the chronicles only become useful when they reach the mid-16th century.

we can reasonably suppose that this is what drove Ponhea Yat's decision to establish his capital at Chaturkukh/Phnom Penh even after he had recaptured Angkor.

CAMBODIA ENTERS THE WORLD

According to the Cambodian chronicles, King Dhammaraja reigned over Cambodia at the very end of the 15th century and into the early 16th century. He was the very model of a Buddhist monarch, one who knew the *tripitaka* (the Buddhist scriptures) by heart and carried out many pious acts. He transferred holy relics of the Buddha from Angkor to a new monastery in Kampong Thom province, gifting male and female slaves for its upkeep and taking the robe himself for three months. The chronicles, which were largely written by monks, depict his reign as a golden age of peace and prosperity.

After the death of Dhammaraja the Khmers fell under an unjust king. There was a man named Kan at court, the son of a low-ranking official and a 'Servant of the Three Jewels', meaning a temple slave. Kan had a beautiful sister, and the king married Kan's sister and awarded his new brother-in-law a high position in the royal palace. Kan saw the king's injustices, raised a rebellion and took the throne.

(The unjust king's name, by the way, was Sugandhapad, and Kan seized the throne in 1512, which puts these events at the very beginning of the European arrival in Southeast Asia. In 1513, just two years after the Portuguese capture of Malacca and a year after Kan's rebellion, King Manuel mentioned to the pope that Cambodia was one of the most powerful states of Further India, and in 1515 the apothecary and ambassador Tome Pires listed the products of the country as lac – a dye – ivory, dried fish and rice, and its imports as Indian textiles, spices, mercury and red beads. Pires describes the king as 'a valiant heathen' who fought with all his neighbours and bowed his head to none, while the Khmer people were warlike and possessed many horses and elephants, and their ships were engaged in trade and piracy, preying on friend and foe alike.)

Kan was now Sdech Kan ('King Kan'), and from his capital at Srei Santhor, a little up the Mekong River from Phnom Penh, he ruled over a Cambodia that stretched north to Laos, west to Ayutthaya, east to Champa and south to the sea. The chronicles say he was a good king, and behind the legends we can even say he was a wealthy and competent one. He was the first since the days of Funan to issue gold and silver coins, and foreigners came to his city to profit from his wisdom and justice. But Sdech Kan was not of royal blood, and for this reason the brother of the former king came from Siam with an army and overthrew him.

The story of Sdech Kan's reign is presumably true in outline if not in its details. What is possibly most interesting about it is that it shows how in

ROYAL REGALIA

The climax of the coronation ceremony comes when the king takes possession of the royal regalia. The most important elements of this are the sword Preah Khan, made by the gods for King Jayavarman VI, a spear once owned by a gardener who ascended the throne upon killing the reigning monarch, and the *kris* (Malay dagger) given to Sultan Ibrahim by his Malay princess. Other important elements include the Great Crown of Victory, the gold betel box and the royal gold slippers.

Several items, including Preah Khan and the Great Crown, have been missing since the overthrow of the monarchy in 1970 (the sword and crown used in coronations since 1993 are replicas). In 1997, a former Lon Nol official claimed that they had been delivered to King Sihanouk in Beijing, but Sihanouk denied having seen them since his overthrow. Another rumour has the Khmer Rouge burying them on the road to the airport, but former KR Head of State Khieu Samphan told the *Phnom Penh Post* in 2004 that the regalia remained in the palace throughout the Khmer Rouge period. The mystery of their disappearance has still to be solved.

Royal enthronements happen only rarely, but in the Throne Hall of the royal palace is a gold statue of King Sisowath sitting on the Preah Thineang Bossabok dressed in the full regalia of kingship.

BELOW: *The royal sword Preah Khan (centre) and its scabbard (top). The blade at the bottom of the picture belongs to the royal lance, another element of the regalia.*

the eyes of the chronicler even a good ruler could not be accepted if he was not descended from the kings of Angkor. Whether the kings whose line was interrupted by Sdech Kan were really connected to Angkor is questionable, but the authors of the chronicles believed they were, and they were making the point that Angkor was what legitimized kingship.

Shortly after Sdech Kan's time, a Portuguese missionary named Gaspar da Cruz visited Cambodia. He recorded that the new king had gained the throne 'because the people rebelled against one of his brothers who was king and he subdued them, therefore his brother gave him the kingdom'. Presumably this refers to the time of Sdech Kan, but Kan himself seems to be absent from the story. The king of Gaspar da Cruz's visit and brother of Sugandhapad was Ang Chan I, who reigned for some 50 years in peace and prosperity. In around 1540 he defeated an invading Siamese army, demonstrating that Cambodia remained a power to be reckoned with.

Gaspar da Cruz came with high hopes of winning souls, but made only

BELOW
Longvek – a Dutch illustration from the mid-17th century.

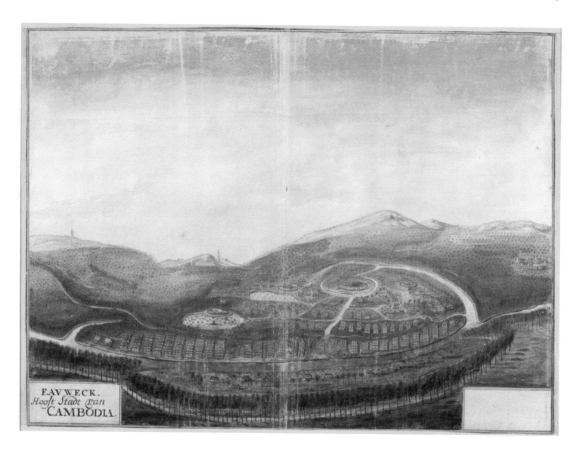

F.AVWECK.
Hooft Stadt van
CAMBODIA.

one convert, who died. The court brahmins were hostile to his presence, the Buddhist monks indifferent and the king had spies everywhere so that ordinary people were afraid to talk to him. He reports on the nations round about, on the close ties between Cambodia, 'Cochin' (southern Vietnam) and China, on how merchants from the three Laotian states travelled down the Mekong River each year to trade with the outside world in Phnom Penh, and on how Luang Prabang was overrun by the Burmese during his stay, disrupting trade between that state and Cambodia. He also describes a trip upriver, where like Zhou Daguan he saw large herds of deer, elephants and rhinoceroses.

Ang Chan's capital was at Longvek, not far up the Tonle Sap River from Phnom Penh. According to the chronicles he was strolling in the nearby forest one day when he saw a large stone caught in the branches of a *koki* tree, whose mystical properties allow it to be planted only by monks and kings. Ang Chan had the tree carved with four Buddhas facing out towards the four points of the compass, while the stone became the plinth for the statue. The four-faced Buddha was the last major iconographic innovation of Cambodian art, and an early example in the shrine of Wat Phnom in Phnom Penh appears to have given that city the name Chaturmukh, 'four faces' (contrary to the tourist guidebooks, the name does not relate to the four rivers joining and separating in front of the royal palace – rivers, in Khmer as in English, have arms, not faces).

Many more stories are told about Ang Chan. He possessed a white elephant that the king of Ayutthaya demanded, as white elephants belong to kings alone. When Ang Chan refused to hand it over the Ayutthayan king attacked Cambodia, but the Khmers won, upon which Ang Chan founded a town on the site and named it Siem Reap, meaning Siam Defeated (the story does not end well for the Cambodians: Ayutthaya attacked again and

ABOVE

Shrine of Wat Phnom, Phnom Penh: the Maitreya Buddha, the fifth, sits in front, and behind him a square pillar with the four previous Buddhas arranged on its four faces. The Sakyamuni Buddha was the most recent historic Buddha, and the coming of the messianic Maitreya Buddha will usher in the end of the current world-age.

ABOVE
Armoured European soldier with an arquebus. The Europeans were consistently ahead of the rest of the world in military innovation, and those Southeast Asian monarchs with the wealth to ensure access to foreign technology gained an edge over their rivals.

OPPOSITE
Bronzes from Angkor in Mandalay. Worshippers rub the belly of this figure to cure stomach complaints.

captured the white elephant). Ang Chan died in 1566. His successor, Paramaraja III, took a Cambodian army to the gates of Ayutthaya in 1569. This was in coordination with the great Burmese conqueror Bayinnaung, who had 80,000 arquebusiers trained by Portuguese mercenaries in target shooting every day, so that 'by continuous exercise they become most excellent shot'. One of the most bizarre, if minor, results of this episode was that a collection of 30 Khmer bronzes originally looted from Angkor in 1431 was taken off to Burma. The last six can be seen today in Mahamuni pagoda in Mandalay, the remainder having been melted down and recast as cannon by King Thibaw in the 19th century to resist the British.

CONQUISTADORES IN CAMBODIA

Paramaraja III was followed by his son, Settha, and in his reign, on 3 January 1594, Longvek fell to Ayutthaya. A Khmer legend tells how the enemy was unable to capture the town because it was surrounded by an impenetrable bamboo forest, but the cunning Siamese loaded their cannon with silver coins and fired them into the bamboo, upon which the Khmers cut down the forest to gather up the coins. The legend implies that Cambodia was defeated by the greed and stupidity of the Khmers themselves. A second story tells of two supernatural brothers, one a wish-granting cow called Preah Ko, the other a handsome prince named Preah Kaev. The two foil the many attempts of the Siamese to take Longvek, but eventually they are captured and carried off into captivity. To this day they remain in Bangkok, weeping unceasingly as they look eastwards towards their homeland, their plight a symbol of the loss of Khmer greatness.

The war began in 1591 with an invasion by King Narasuan, who had restored Ayutthaya's independence after the Burmese invasion. King Settha repelled the attack and a renewed threat from Burma forced Narasuan to turn his attention back to the west, but when this had been dealt with he led another army into Cambodia. Settha's army of 75,000 men and 150

war junks was commanded by his brother, Prince Suryopear, but despite Suryopear's dogged resistance Longvek fell. According to Thai chronicles, 90,000 Cambodians were taken into captivity, including Suryopear. Commoners were put to work on irrigation projects, but Suryopear was kept at the court in Ayutthaya.

Events before and after the fall of Longvek illustrate the quite disproportionate impact of European military technology on Southeast Asian politics in this period. In 1592, two Spanish adventurers, Blas Ruiz and Gregorio de Vargas, set off from Guangzhou in a Chinese junk bound for Cambodia. In Champa the king seized their ship and cargo, but they managed to continue onwards and arrived in Longvek the next year. There they befriended Diogo Veloso, a Portuguese who had married the daughter of King Settha. This king was preparing his defences against Narasuan at the time, and on the advice of the visitors he wrote to the governor of Manila seeking Spanish help, offering in return trading privileges and the right to proselytize freely in the kingdom.

Veloso and Vargas set off for Manila with Settha's letter in June 1593. They returned early in 1594 with a vague promise of support, but found that Longvek had already fallen and Settha had fled to Laos. Cambodia was in turmoil. Veloso, Ruiz and Vargas made their various ways back to Manila, which they reached after many adventures.

In January 1596, Veloso and Ruiz returned to Phnom Penh without Vargas but accompanied by conquistadores and friars, to find that a minor noble named Ream, a man of ability of the type that emerges again and again in such situations in Southeast Asian history, had reunified the country. Ream had set up his court in Srei Santhor, but Phnom Penh was still the commercial capital. The town reportedly held 20,000 households, suggesting a population of perhaps 50,000, but the Australian historian Milton Osborne, who records this in his book *Phnom Penh: A Cultural and Literary History*, feels that this is much too high and that 10,000 is more likely. The town was highly cosmopolitan, with the 3,000 Chinese living alongside Muslim Chams, Malays and Catholic Japanese, the last being refugees from the anti-Christian persecutions of the Japanese court.

Ream distrusted the visitors and they distrusted him. Tensions rose, and the Spanish attacked the Chinese, burnt their ships and killed several hundred people. Forty conquistadores marched to Srei Santhor, where they murdered the king and his family, massacred the inhabitants and torched the town. Their chronicler, the Spanish friar Diego Aduarte, described the scene as 'like Rome burning, Troy annihilated, or Carthage destroyed'.

Vargas arrived shortly afterwards and was appalled at what his compatriots had done. He returned to Manila, and Veloso and Ruiz travelled to Laos to retrieve Settha. They found that he had died the previous year, so they brought his son back with a Lao army, put him on the throne as Borom Reachea, and made themselves governors of provinces with all that went with it in terms of control over trade and levies.

While Veloso and Ruiz enriched themselves, Borom Reachea failed to gain the support of the Khmer nobles, and rebels multiplied. The most powerful was a Malay from Johore who went by the name, or rather title, Laksamana, meaning the Admiral, a reference to the fleet of fast prahus with which he controlled the rivers. He also commanded a large force of artillery and 4,000 Muslim Malays and Chams, all deeply hostile to the Portuguese

and Spanish in view of the cruel treatment the Catholics meted out to Muslims in Asia. Veloso and Ruiz called on Manila for reinforcements, and in mid-1599 two shiploads of desperadoes and friars dropped anchor near the Muslim quarter of Phnom Penh. The Malays, Chams, Japanese and Khmers joined together to slaughter them and burn their ships, leaving Ruiz and Veloso among the dead. Laksamana killed Borom Reachea and made himself de facto ruler of eastern Cambodia until the Khmer nobles organized an army and killed him.

ALARMS AND EXCURSIONS

Eight years after the fall of Longvek, Cambodia was ruled by Banna Nom, a boy of 18 who failed to observe the Ten Royal Virtues, drank alcohol and indulged in hunting. Without virtue in the king, the kingdom was afflicted by drought and famine, tigers entered the villages and a meteor fell on the royal palace. The obnoxious teenager's grandmother, concerned for the future of the Khmer race, called on the king of Ayutthaya to intervene. By good fortune there was at that time in Ayutthaya a pious and devout monk, Suryopear by name, who was of ancient royal blood, so Cambodia was saved (the unfortunate Banna Nom was tied in a sack and thrown into the river at Phnom Penh, thus avoiding the sin of shedding royal blood).

Suryopear had been placed in charge of the royal elephants in Ayutthaya, a prestigious position, and he is still remembered as the author of an important textbook on their classification. After swearing his loyalty to the king of

Ayutthaya, he took the throne of Cambodia in 1602 and began the reconstruction of the kingdom. He protected and promoted Buddhism, donating Buddha images and slaves to important monasteries and reforming the hierarchy, and was also mindful of the financial basis of kingship, appointing the abbot of Wat Sambok in Kratie province to collect dues and tariffs from boats bringing forest products down the Mekong River. In 1618, in his old age, he abdicated in favour of his son Chey Chettha II and entered a monastery, where he died the next year. All the chronicles agree that his was a reign of stability, prosperity and peace.

An important event that occurred at about this time was the marriage of Chey Chetta to a daughter of Nguyen Phuoc Nguyen, the ruler of the southern half of Vietnam. The marriage is important not for its influence on the course of Cambodian history, for it had none, but because modern Khmers remember Chey Chettha as the king who gave the town of Prey Nokor to the Nguyen, thus beginning the loss of Kampuchea Krom to the Vietnamese. Prey Nokor is known today as Ho Chi Minh City, but it still appears under its Khmer name on Cambodian maps. A more sophisticated variation of the story, one that does not regard the marriage to the Vietnamese princess as historically significant, is that Chey Chettha granted the Vietnamese the right to establish settlements around Prey Nokor in return for help against the threat of invasion from Ayutthaya.

In both versions of the story, the loss of Prey Nokor and the reign of Chey Chettha were the beginning of Cambodia's historic weakness in the face of its aggressive neighbours, but historians are increasingly coming to the view that Chey Chettha has been maligned, that Cambodia continued to be the military equal of both Vietnam and Ayutthaya until the middle of the 17th century, and that this marriage, like dynastic marriages everywhere, was intended to seal a military alliance between two rulers.

Of the two, Chey Chettha and Nguyen Phuoc Nguyen, it was Nguyen who was in the weaker position. He had recently declared his independence from the emperor in Hanoi, but Hanoi had far greater reserves of manpower and could mobilize an army of 100,000 men, 500 elephants and 500 ships. Nguyen had Portuguese military advisors who had helped him build two massive walls stretching from the sea to the mountains, and was defending it with the latest European cannon, but he desperately needed elephants, and Cambodia had been recognized for centuries as a source of trained war

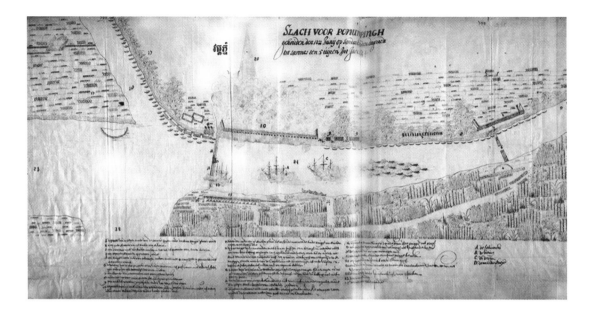

SLACH VOOR PONUMPINGH

In 1664 five Dutch ships went to teach the King of Cambodia a lesson, but suffered an ignominious defeat. Only three escaped. Phnom Penh, 12 June 1664. (Map held in the National Archive, the Hague.)

elephants. In return he offered Chey Chettha his support against Cambodia's traditional enemy, Ayutthaya.

Christoforo Borri, a Jesuit missionary in Nguyen's capital at Hue, records that the king was 'in constant motion, and making warlike preparations to assist the king of Cambogia who has married his bastard daughter, sending him succours of galleys and men against the king of Siam...' In 1622, Ayutthaya attacked by land and sea, but Chey Chettha fought off the invaders. There was a second invasion the next year, and again Chey Chettha was victorious. The significance of these victories, and also of the alliance between Chey Chettha and the Nguyen of southern Vietnam, is that they demonstrate Cambodia holding its own in the world of mainland Southeast Asian politics, able to fight off invasions by the Siamese and being treated as a respected equal by the Vietnamese.

On Chey Chettha's death in 1628, the nobles offered the throne to his younger brother, Outhei, who had been with him in captivity in Ayutthaya, but Outhei declined and took instead the position of *obbareach* (Second King, sometimes but inaccurately translated as regent), while Chey Chettha's son, Chau Bunna Tu, became king. This was far from unprecedented – there was an almost exact parallel in Ayutthaya at the same time, where Phya Si Worawong manipulated a series of child kings while acting as the real power behind the throne, but while Phya Si Worawong had little choice, having only a weak claim to the throne, Outhei could have become king in his own right.

This was a uniquely favoured period in Cambodia's relations with its neighbours. The Nguyen were still occupied in their war with the Trinh in the north and continued to value Cambodia as an ally, and Ayutthaya lacked the resources to send another campaign against its neighbour. Phnom Penh continued to be an important port, with thriving foreign communities including Portuguese, Spanish, Dutch, Malays, Chams, Persians, Arabs, Chinese and Japanese. The most important were the Dutch and the Malays, bitter commercial rivals, the latter enjoying a fearsome military reputation.

Dutch visitors of the period reported that Cambodia had an Old King and a Young King, of whom the Old King was the more powerful. Bunna Tu chaffed against his uncle's control, rebelled and was killed. Outhei was again offered the throne and again refused, and it was given instead to Bunna Nur, another son of Chey Chettha. Bunna Nur died under mysterious circumstances in 1640 and was followed by Padumaraja, a son of Outhei. Chey Chettha had a third son, one who had been passed over when Padumaraja was made king. In 1642, with the support of the Malays and Chams, he murdered both Padumaraja and Outhei. At first he reigned as a Buddhist king under the name Ramadhipati, but later – just when is uncertain – he converted to Islam and adopted the name Sultan Ibrahim.

The reasons for his conversion are much debated. According to popular Cambodian legend a beautiful Cham princess ensnared him with magic potions. His marriage to a Cham princess was real enough, but Western historians are inclined to think that both it and the conversion were the result of cold, hard calculation – a desire to cement the loyalty of the Malays and Chams who had put him on the throne, and whose support gave him access to the extensive trade of the Malays. A third possibility, supported by a few passages in the chronicles and by comments from contemporary Westerners, is that the king was half mad with guilt over the murder of his uncle and cousin, for he had carried these out with his own hands. The chronicles tell how Ramadhipati consulted the monks to ask how the guilt of murder could be wiped out, and was told that it could not; he then went to the Muslim holy men and was told that it could. Whatever his motives and aims, on his conversion he replaced the high officials of the court with Muslims and forced his nobles to accept circumcision.

Meanwhile the Japanese government had banned all except Chinese and Dutch shipping from its markets, but Portuguese traders in Phnom Penh were avoiding the ban by conspiring with the Chinese and Japanese communities to send their Cambodian cargoes on Chinese junks. The Japan trade was highly profitable for the Dutch, and tensions rose. In 1641, a Portuguese murdered a Dutch boatswain in Phnom Penh, and in September 1643, following further incidents, Pieter van Regesmortes, the Chief Merchant, travelled to the court at Udong to protest. Van Regesmortes was an insolent man and Sultan Ibrahim was a hot-tempered one, and Ibrahim had van Regesmortes and the entire Dutch commercial community murdered. Next year, five Dutch ships sailed up the Mekong River to punish Ibrahim, but instead suffered an ignominious defeat that ended the Dutch presence in Cambodia.

Sultan Ibrahim remained on the throne for 15 years, far longer than the average for the century and an indication that he was far from mad or incompetent. Eventually two sons of Outhei launched a revolt, and as Ibrahim had the support of the Malays, Japanese and Portuguese, the brothers appealed to Nguyen Hien Vuong, the king of Hue, for military support. The Vietnamese invaded, the rebels won and Ibrahim was taken to Hue in a cage, where he died in captivity in 1659 and was given a proper Buddhist-style cremation.

Ang Sor, the elder of the two sons of Outhei, reigned for 12 years and was assassinated by his nephew, who was also his son-in-law. The nephew-cum-son-in-law reigned for a year and was assassinated, and in 1673–1679 there was another Vietnamese intervention. The next 20 years were very similar.

THE COMING OF THE CHINESE

While Cambodia sank into a round of rebellions and assassinations, significant events were happening in the wider world. In China the Ming dynasty was overthrown by the Manchus, and Manchu suppression of the last remnants of Ming opposition led to an exodus of refugees to Southeast Asia. In 1680 a shipload of these arrived in Cambodia and they were allowed to settle at a port town a little eastwards from Kep. This place, called in Khmer Banteay Meas, had a singular geographic advantage: every winter the inland plain flooded and it became possible to sail from Ha Tien, as it became known, to Phnom Penh via a deep, narrow river. In the 18th century, Ha

Tien developed into a quasi-independent city-state famous for its prosperity and freedom from royal monopolies, and it remained the main seaport for Cambodia into the early 19th century.

Chinese refugees also turned up in Hue, and the Nguyen encouraged them to settle in the south. In 1698/99 two new provinces were created, Bien Hoa and Gia Dinh, and Saigon became part of the Nguyen domains. Cambodia's loss of Saigon can be dated to this event, but it was not the disaster for Cambodia that it seems looking backwards from our own age, when Ho Chi Minh City and Bangkok dominate the region. That primacy became established only in the late 19th century, but through the 18th century and well into the 19th century, trade was carried out through a constellation of little ports like Ha Tien, Chanthaburi, Kampot and Bassac, the last being the most important town in the delta in the 1760s. Nor was the political status of ports as clear-cut as such things are today: control of Bassac, for example (today's Soc Trang), was shared four ways by a local warlord, the Nguyen, the King of Cambodia and the King of Siam, none of them able to claim complete ownership.

Nevertheless, there was a definite decay of Cambodia's sovereignty after the second half of the 17th century. This had many causes, but partly it was because the political system was based on royal patronage, each new reign bringing a new set of patron-client relations, with little if any continuity with what had gone before. This recurring turmoil was exacerbated by the lack of clear rules or conventions for royal succession: all princes had equal claims, any claim rested on the assent of the *oknhas* and each king cemented himself in power by buying them off. To do this he needed control of trade, which also gave him control of military power. Rivals consisting of other princes backed by out-of-favour factions of the elite, lacking access to military power themselves, went to those who could provide it, which meant the Thais and Vietnamese.

This brings up the question of the structure of Cambodian society. At the broad level it was divided between the elite and the commoners. The elite included the king and his court, important families in the provinces, wealthy merchant families in the capital and the trading towns, and important monks. They had close ties with the very similar elite in Ayutthaya, with monks, traders and officials passing constantly to and fro even when political relations were at their most tense. Relations with the Vietnamese elite

A 19th-century engraving of a scene in the Delta.

were less close, largely due to the difference in culture, but they were real and played an important part in Cambodia's history.

VIETNAM AND THE DELTA

Vietnamese settlement in the delta began in earnest after the war between the Nguyen and Trinh ended in 1673. By 1700, some 40,000 households had settled there, but good land was scarce and tensions between the immigrants and the established Khmer inevitably rose. In 1731, they exploded in an attack on Ha Tien, led by an ex-monk and supported by Khmer officials. The uprising soon engulfed the entire delta, and a French missionary reported that the rebels 'killed all those (Vietnamese) that they found in Cambodia, men, women and children'. The Nguyen blamed the Cambodian king and launched two attacks against him, but at the end the Cambodians retained control of most of the delta.

In 1749, King Ang Snguon came to the throne at Udong, and the next year another slaughter of Vietnamese settlers broke out. French missionaries reported that the Cambodians

have massacred all the Cochinchinese (Vietnamese) . . . At first they took
no prisoners, but killed all those they could find. Now they are sent as slaves
to the king of Siam, to repay him for the help he has given to the king of
Cambodia.

A little later they reported that the killings had been organized by Ang
Snguon himself, with the wholehearted support of his court. There was yet
another massacre of Vietnamese in 1769.

Yet the depth and extent of ethnic antipathy between Khmers and
Vietnamese should not be exaggerated. In long-settled areas intermar-
riage was not uncommon, and cultural assimilation provoked complaints
from later Vietnamese emperors that Vietnamese villagers were becoming Khmerized. Nevertheless, the intense fear and hatred that modern
Cambodians feel towards Vietnam and ethnic Vietnamese can be traced
back to the 18th century, and especially to its second half.

CAMBODIA'S NEAR-DEATH EXPERIENCE

In 1767, Ayutthaya was razed to the ground by the Burmese and its royal
family extinguished. It might have seemed that Cambodia would have a
small respite from bullying by its powerful neighbour, but within a year a
former provincial governor named Taksin restored the kingdom, and the
contest between Siam and Vietnam resumed.

In 1769, the Nguyen deposed the current Cambodian king and replaced him with his brother, who refused to pay tribute to Taksin in his
new capital at Bangkok. Taksin responded by occupying Battambang and
Siem Reap, the Vietnamese retaliated by raiding Trat and Chanthaburi, and
Taksin launched a land and sea invasion via Ha Tien that returned Siam's
protégé to the throne. The situation seemed bound to escalate, but the
Nguyen became increasingly distracted by an internal rebellion and made
peace with Bangkok. The rebels quickly gained ground, and in 1776 the last
Nguyen stronghold fell to them. The most senior survivor of the massacre
of the royal family that followed was a boy of 15 named Nguyen Anh, who
immediately set about raising an army.

In Cambodia the royal clan and the *oknhas* were divided between pro-
Taksin, pro-Nguyen and pro-rebel factions. In 1779, a senior pro-Siamese
oknha named Baen sent the five-year-old Ang Eng to Bangkok for his safety.

Taksin was killed shortly afterwards and succeeded by Rama I, the first king of the Chakri dynasty that still rules Thailand. Rama treated Ang Eng as his own son, and in 1794 he was brought back to Cambodia and crowned at Udong. 'The sky did not darken, nor did rain fall, but thunder boomed in the sky at noon with the noise of a mighty storm', rejoiced the Royal Chronicle. The Siamese army that brought Ang Eng back was commanded by Baen, who declared himself Lord Governor of Battambang and Angkor on behalf of Rama I. Baen settled in at Battambang as an independent prince, and the western provinces were lost to Cambodia for the next two centuries.

Ang Eng's reign was brief, uneventful and closely monitored by Rama's representatives at his court. He built a new palace at Udong, visited Bangkok in 1796 to present tribute and died the next year, leaving behind four sons, all under age. Ang Chan II, the eldest and heir apparent, was brought up under close Siamese supervision. He ascended the throne in 1806, receiving the crown in Bangkok, full of resentment against the Siamese.

By this time Nguyen Anh had defeated the rebels, and reunified north and south Vietnam for the first time in centuries. He adopted the name Gia Long, meaning 'Prosperity', but recalling Gia Dịnh (Saigon) and Thang Long (Hanoi), and in 1804 the Chinese court permitted him to take the title of Emperor. It must have seemed to Ang Chan that the new Vietnamese ruler represented a way out from Siamese overlordship, and he began to distance himself from Bangkok. He voluntarily sought out Gia Long as his suzerain almost immediately on becoming king, failed to attend the cremation of Rama I in 1809, and a little later broke a core obligation of the vassal-suzerain relationship by refusing to send Cambodian troops to help in a campaign against Burma.

These were provocations Bangkok could not ignore. Rama I had died, but Rama II reaffirmed the annexation of Battambang and Siem Reap, and began moves to extend his control into adjacent provinces. At his prompting the governor of Kampong Svay, the modern Kampong Thom, refused to swear the usual oath of loyalty to the king. Ang Chan had him assassinated. In 1812, Ang Chan's brother, Ang Snguon (not to be confused with the earlier king of the same name), fled to Battambang and demanded to be named *obbareach* (Second King) with control of half the country. Ang Chan refused. Rama II sent an army to support Ang Sgnuon, who had been joined by his two younger brothers, and the Thais quickly overran Cambodia. Ang

Chan retreated to Saigon and appealed to Gia Long, who sent a Vietnamese army that quickly defeated the Siamese. Neither Rama nor Gia Long wished to go to war, so the two reached an agreement to share suzerainty over Cambodia, the King of Siam as the 'father' and the Emperor of Vietnam as the 'mother'.

So peace was restored, but the Siamese held the west and north, and the east was a Vietnamese protectorate. Gia Long stated that 'the purpose of the institution of the protectorate is to strengthen the preservation' of Cambodia, and ordered his officials in Phnom Penh to ensure that the Cambodian court retained its autonomy. In 1820 he died and was followed by his son, the Emperor Minh Mang. The new emperor was of a different temperament to his father – less flexible, less tolerant and more insensitive to the possible adverse consequences of his policies. Nevertheless, he began

by regarding the Cambodian king as a kind of little brother, one who could be educated and brought up to responsibility.

The ship of good intentions hit the iceberg of reality at the Vinh Te canal. The Vietnamese rulers were great promotors of canal building, and Vinh Te had much in its favour. Linking Ha Tien to Chau Doc some 70km (44 miles) away, it would drain swamps, improve communications, open up farmland and make everyone better off. Ang Chan had been involved in the planning, as it would run through Khmer-populated areas, and the work gangs were to be made up of equal numbers of Khmers and Vietnamese, since both Khmers and Vietnamese would share in the benefits.

Work began in 1820, but soon Minh Mang received reports that the Cambodians were deserting the project. He ordered that prayers be offered and medicine be distributed, and that burials should be at public expense, and asked Ang Chan to explain to the Khmers that while their present labour was hard, future generations would reap the rewards.

Minh Mang seems to have been genuinely sympathetic within the constraints of his extremely rigid personality, but Vietnamese officials on the ground were far more high-handed. Resentment grew, the Khmer continued to desert and eventually work had to be suspended. The shambles confirmed national stereotypes on each side, for the Vietnamese that the Khmer were lazy and unreliable, for the Cambodians that the Vietnamese were arrogant and cruel.

The canal also sparked a major rebellion, led by a magical ex-monk named Kai who declared himself king, attracted a rabble army of peasant followers and massacred Vietnamese throughout eastern Cambodia. A celebrated poem written 50 years later by another monk, Pich, relates how the soil was soaked in blood and the dead lay everywhere. But as Pich points out, Kai lost his store of merit by taking life, and he was defeated by a Vietnamese army near Kampong Cham. The Vietnamese must have seen this interlude as yet another example of Khmer backwardness, but for Cambodians like Pich, Kai and his followers were answering a call for national survival.

Rama III had come to the throne in Bangkok in 1824, and was growing increasingly concerned about Vietnamese expansion. Minh Mang was meddling in Laos, which Siam regarded as its own territory, and the court of Cambodia was being steadily purged of pro-Siamese *oknhas*. Rama determined to end what he termed this 'Vietnamese insolence and contempt' towards Siam. His opportunity came in 1833, when Minh Mang's customary insensitivity provoked a serious rebellion in the delta that united Catholic Vietnamese, Muslim Cham and the Chinese of Saigon as well as Khmers. The rebel leader called on Bangkok for support, and Rama III ordered his best general, Chaophraya Bodin, to evict the Vietnamese from Cambodia, or if that proved not to be possible, to depopulate the country so that it became a lifeless wilderness.

Bodin set out in November 1833, aiming to seize Phnom Penh and proceed to Saigon. Ang Snguon had died, but he took with him the two remaining brothers of Ang Chan, Ang Im and Ang Duong, intending to place them together on the throne. Ang Chan and the outnumbered Vietnamese abandoned Phnom Penh and Bodin advanced deep into the delta, but in February 1834 his army was routed. The second part of his instructions then became operative, and as he retreated he torched towns and villages in his path and deported entire populations. Ang Chan, returning with the Vietnamese army, died aboard the royal barge at Phnom Penh in sight of his burnt-out palace.

The throne was now vacant, and Ang Im and Ang Duong immediately

BELOW
The Vinh Te canal, connecting the port of Ha Tien to Chau Doc on the Bassac branch of the Mekong.

laid claim to it. Minh Mang held the advantage in many ways, including having the better army and possession of the royal regalia without which no Khmer king could have legitimacy, but what he did not have was a male candidate to the throne, for Ang Chan had left only daughters. The eldest was too pro-Siamese, so the second was crowned as Queen Ang Mei, the first Khmer queen since Jayadevi. She and her sisters were assigned Vietnamese titles and Vietnamese bodyguards, the former to integrate them into the Vietnamese bureaucratic hierarchy, the latter ostensibly for their protection, but in reality to prevent them from running off to join the Siamese, who were threatening a renewed invasion.

Minh Mang now had good reason to be deeply concerned about this possibility, for Rama was massing troops in the west and had installed Ang Im and Ang Duong there as provincial governors, positions they could use to forge links with the *oknhas* in the east. Up to this point his rule in Cambodia had been relatively mild, but the invasion forced him to conclude that eastern Cambodia, and for that matter the delta with its large Khmer population, could never be secure until the Khmer became civilized, meaning less like Thais and more like Vietnamese. 'We must hope that their barbarian habits will be subconsciously dissipated, and that they will daily become more accustomed to Han [Vietnamese] ways.'

Ang Mei was queen in name only, for the government lay in the hands of the viceroy, Truong Minh Giang. The viceroy saw many issues that needed addressing, such as the lack of a professional Cambodian standing army to keep the Siamese at bay, and the fact that less than half the land was under cultivation, with even that given over to cotton and betel nuts instead of rice. He set to work, but soon discovered that the Khmer officials on whom he had to rely were corrupt and incompetent, and could not be

BELOW
The Emperor Minh Mang.

brought to understand that they should not buy and sell their positions. Underlying these faults was a failure of morals. 'They do not know the ethical codes. Although they accept the supreme power of our country, they still keep their own customs.'

The Viceroy set about addressing these deficiencies. Court officials were required to appear before their Vietnamese superiors in Vietnamese costume every morning to deliver reports and receive their daily instructions, and the civil administration was reorganized along Vietnamese lines, with the country divided into districts each administered by a Vietnamese military official seconded by a Cambodian *oknha*. The Cambodian army was modernized and placed under Vietnamese control, and strengthened with one Vietnamese soldier to every four Khmers, while masses of Cambodians were drafted into labour gangs to work on public projects.

ABOVE

Chaophraya Bodin (Bodindecha), the Siamese general who played a major role in the Siamese-Vietnamese wars of 1831–34 and 1841–1845.

These things could perhaps be understood if not accepted, but Khmer culture itself was to be remade. Place names were changed from Khmer to Vietnamese (Phnom Penh became Tran Tray, 'Western Commandery'), Khmer women were ordered to grow their hair long and to wear trousers in the Vietnamese style, and only Vietnamese food was allowed to be sold in the markets. Monasteries were emptied of monks, sacred images were destroyed and the funeral monuments of departed ancestors that line monastery walls were dismantled. Far from least, 5,000 Vietnamese were settled each year on Cambodian land. The Cambodians, in view of the bright Vietnamese future that awaited them, were to be called *tan dan*, meaning New People.

Not surprisingly, these policies provoked resistance. *Oknha* led their people in local revolts or into exile in Battambang, and at least one was executed for refusing to implement the Vietnamization policy. This ingratitude left the emperor infuriated and bewildered. He had '[brought] the

123

Cambodian people out of the mud and into a warm feather bed ... why are there people who hate us and believe the rebels?'

The situation took a dramatic turn in 1840, when it was discovered that the pro-Siamese elder sister of Ang Mei was planning an escape to Battambang. She was imprisoned and charged with collaborating with the enemy, while the queen and royal court were whisked off to Saigon. A Siamese chronicle describes what happened next:

> *On the third day of the waning moon of the ninth month (16 August 1840) all oknha agreed to plot against the Vietnamese in every town and city. The Cambodians arrested the Vietnamese soldiers ... many Vietnamese throughout the country were killed ... Vietnamese military chiefs were unable to quell the rebellion ...*

The uprising led swiftly to the intervention of a mixed Siamese-Khmer army from Battambang under the command of Bodin. With him came Ang Duong, now the sole remaining Siamese claimant to the Cambodian throne, Ang Im having defected to the Vietnamese side (Minh Mang, who had no time for traitors, immediately had him imprisoned, and he later died). Bodin's mission was one of liberation, but as he wrote to Rama III, 'the final aim is to take over, no matter what, the control of the Cambodian country and its people'.

Minh Mang died in January 1841, and in April, in an attempt to appease the rebels, his successor Thieu Tri reinstalled Ang Mei as queen in Phnom Penh. Two days later, Bodin and Ang Duong and their mixed Siamese-Khmer army reached Udong, and the Vietnamese abandoned Phnom Penh, taking Ang Mei with them.

For some years the Siamese and Ang Duang held Udong and Phnom Penh, but they were at a distinct disadvantage with their long supply lines stretching back to Battambang, while Vietnam lay just down the river from Phnom Penh. In 1845, Thieu Tri sent an army of 20,000 men and 1,000 war junks against them. He recaptured Phnom Penh and encircled Udong, but proved unable to take it. Bodin reported to Rama III,

> *the Khmer fighters have nearly all perished. The soldiers are afraid of the Vietnamese, the population have fled into the forest to find food, the*

fields are uncultivated, and Cambodia knows famine ... [A] good number of Khmers [have] rallied to Annam (the Vietnamese side) for the sake of peace.

Thieu Tri, for his part, was faced with the increasingly bellicose behaviour of French warships off his coast in support of Vietnamese Catholics, and was now eager to end involvement in Cambodia. Negotiations began early in 1846 and a treaty was signed in 1847. Its main points were that all foreign troops should withdraw from Cambodian territory, Siam retaining Battambang, Siem Reap and the northern provinces as far as the Mekong River, and Vietnam giving up Kampot, which it had assimilated some decades earlier. Ang Duong and Ang Mei were to be joint monarchs, sending tribute every year to Bangkok and every three years to Hue. Simultaneous coronations were held in Udong and Hue in April 1848.

The joint monarchy quickly turned into the sole monarchy of Ang Duong, who went on to be one of the most revered of modern Khmer monarchs. Ang Mei is reviled today as a Vietnamese puppet when remembered at all. She died in Udong in 1874, and a French visitor who saw her shortly before her death described her as 'old ... and mad ... long since removed from power and the world ... almost alone in the furthest corner of the old capital'.

THE KINGDOM SAVED

With the kingdom saved, old traditions reasserted themselves. Ang Duong sent his sons to Bangkok for their further education (a very real benefit, as Bangkok, unlike Udong, was open to the world), and not coincidentally to develop bonds of personal loyalty to the Chakri dynasty. A senior Siamese official resided at Udong to ensure that Ang Duong did not stray from the will of Bangkok, and when the new king needed to fill a number of important posts, including that of *talaha* (prime minister), he dutifully passed the decision to King Rama.

Vietnamese peasants began migrating into the delta in large numbers now that peace had been restored. The 19th-century colonial French historian Adhémard Leclère described them as 'quarrelsome troublemakers' who made life 'impossible' for the Khmers, and many Khmer farmers were abandoning their fields and moving to Ang Duong's lands. The border remained porous and ill defined, and Ang Duong never accepted the situation as final.

Lacking the authority to assert himself against Bangkok or in the delta, Ang Duong could still address the restoration of Khmer-ness. He rebuilt the sangha and constructed monasteries, and restored a distinctively Khmer court protocol that revitalized the pride of both *oknhas* and people in their king. He spent much time in ritual duties that emphasized the connection between the king, the people and the land, such as the Royal Ploughing Ceremony, annual boat races and Khmer New Year celebrations. The tradition linking kingship with national fortune was still very much alive well into the post-Khmer Rouge period, when an old farmer told a visiting foreign journalist that Cambodia had had no good luck since the king (he meant Sihanouk) was overthrown.

This was not the end of Ang Doung's reconstitution of the nation, although it probably ranked very high both for his people and with the king himself. He fostered traditional culture, especially court dance, and as a poet and historian he oversaw a flowering of Cambodian literature. In 1837, he wrote the *Chbab Srey*, a work instructing girls on proper behaviour becoming to their sex. Possibly he was provoked by Ang Mei's role in blocking his path to the throne, but it is a profoundly misogynistic document, the essential idea being that a wife must be totally submissive to her husband. If her husband beats her she should not tell anyone, not even her mother; if he takes a mistress she should not be angry or upset; if he becomes angry she should forgive him, even if the fault is his. It is debatable how much influence the *Chbab Srey* ever really had over Cambodian society, but as of 2015 a condensed version was still being taught to school students.

Ang Duong attempted a restoration, not a revolution. As David Chandler, the pre-eminent historian of modern Cambodia, has commented, 19th-century Cambodia resembled Angkor more closely than a modern centralized state like France, China or Vietnam (or, he could have added, Siam). The authority of the king was based on his personal bonds with the *oknha*, to whom he gave high-sounding titles and the right to milk the nation's revenues, and in return they gave him a fickle sort of loyalty. If his reign was peaceful it was because he was the last prince left standing after decades of war, so faced no jealous rival.

The fact was that the kingdom was destitute, its population ravaged by death and mass deportations, its agriculture destroyed, its access to foreign commerce non-existent. The treasury was bankrupt. Ang Duong was aware of the problem. With the only asset still available to him, corvée labour, he built a road to the port of Kampot to avoid the Vietnamese monopoly of the Mekong River. He reduced taxes and imported a modern coin press to stimulate trade and markets. He urged his subjects to educate their children, and helped the monks to set up schools in the country's monasteries. In very many ways he deserves the high reputation he enjoys.

In 1853, on the advice of Bishop Jean-Claude Miche, the head of the French Catholics in Cambodia, Ang Duong wrote to Napoleon III, recently installed as Emperor of France. The letter has disappeared, and this is most unfortunate as the king's intentions are the centre of an unresolved dispute: was he after a French protectorate, or was he simply seeking to open diplomatic relations? Even the second would be a major breach of protocol with his overlords in Bangkok.

For some time the French did nothing, but in 1856 Napoleon despatched Charles de Montigny, a veteran diplomat, on a mission to Hue to demand reparations for the Vietnamese harassment of Catholic converts. De Montigny took the opportunity to call in at Bangkok to discuss trade issues with King Rama IV (King Mongkut), and in the course of the conversation he casually mentioned that Ang Duong's presents to

BELOW
King Ang Duong, from a stamp issued by the French.

THE ROAD TO UDONG

Henri Mouhot's description of the first day of his journey from Kampot to Udong.

It is reckoned an eight-days' journey travelling with oxen or buffaloes, and there are eight stations on the way. With elephants you can accomplish it in half the time; but only the king, the mandarins, and very wealthy persons can afford to keep these animals. The conveyances which I had engaged could scarcely hold my baggage, so that my men were obliged to make the journey on foot. ...

After traversing a marshy plain, where we knocked down several aquatic birds, we entered a beautiful forest, which stretches unbroken to the very gates of Udong. ... [O]wing to the dry weather and the constant communication between Komput and the capital, the road was almost everywhere in good condition. The heat was intense, and our progress excessively slow; but at length we reached the first station, where I was lodged in a large hall, thatched and built of bamboo, which had been erected for the accommodation of the king and his suite. At night, guards were stationed at my door to protect me from robbery; and, thanks to the royal letter which I carried, I was respectfully treated. On the following morning I managed, at the cost of a franc of our money, to hire an elephant to take me as far as the next station.

BELOW

*Villa of Napoleon III built
in 1866 for the opening of
the Suez Canal and given
next year to King Norodom.
For some time it was
Norodom's favourite palace,
and a lasting sign of French
Imperial friendship to the
Cambodian monarch.*

Napoleon had unfortunately not yet been received. Rama was shocked: he knew nothing of this.

From Bangkok, de Montigny sailed to Kampot, Cambodia's sole port, intending to travel on by land to Udong. Siamese officials from the Khmer court met him in Kampot and dissuaded him from his plan: the journey was difficult, there were no respectable rest houses, he should wait and the king would come to Kampot. After a week of waiting a message arrived from Ang Duong: the king had fallen victim to a painful attack of boils and could not come, but he was sending his prime minister with 200 elephants to escort the French delegation to Udong.

The prime minister arrived, and de Montigny informed him that his objective was to open the country to trade and to missionaries. De Montigny presented a draft convention, under which Cambodia would concede to France what amounted to a monopoly on trade, while missionaries would have the right to build churches 'in any place'. In principle this would allow a church to be erected next to every monastery in the country. Nowhere was there any mention of what Cambodia might expect in return. De Montigny left Kampot on 22 October, confident of success. He was astonished to receive word in due course that the king had refused to sign.

Ang Duong seemed content with things as they were, but years later, in the days of the French Protectorate, a courtier who had known him well told Adhémard Leclère that in his heart the king had regarded both Vietnam and Siam as enemies intent on the kingdom's destruction. 'We should not look to recover what has been taken from us, but only to look after what has been left.' He had no confidence in the survival of a friendless Cambodia.

5

COLONIAL KINGDOM
From the Protectorate to the fall of Sihanouk
1860–1970

Ang Duong died in the winter of 1860. Like previous kings he had many wives, and like them he left behind many sons, of whom three were to play significant roles in the next half-century. Wishing to avoid the chaos that had followed his father's death, he had already designated the eldest of his sons, Prince Norodom, as his heir, and a delegation was sent immediately to Bangkok to inform King Rama IV. This was purely a formality, as Rama had established the succession by decree some years earlier.

OPPOSITE
Independence Monument, Phnom Penh, designed by architect Van Molyvann.

BELOW
King Norodom.

THE KING IN PERIL

Cambodians might reasonably have hoped that they could look forward to the first peaceful transition in many decades. It was not to be, for when

the delegation returned it was accompanied by Norodom's 19-year-old half-brother, Prince Sivotha, who felt that he should be king. Failing to find support among the *oknha* of Udong, he prevailed instead upon a maternal uncle to raise a revolt in the eastern provinces on his behalf. The administration responded feebly, the rebels seized Phnom Penh and Norodom was dismayed to find that he was unable to muster the support to oppose them. He fled to Battambang, then Bangkok, leaving his more popular half-brother, Prince Sisowath, to hold Udong for him.

Rama IV seriously considered dethroning Norodom and replacing him with Sisowath, 'an honest man and much loved by the people', but his advisors warned him that Sisowath's popularity would give him an independent base of

131

support in Cambodia, while Norodom's lack of a following meant that he would remain reliant on Bangkok. Siamese troops brought Norodom back to Udong, and by the end of 1862 the insurrection had been put down.

If Sivotha's revolt had taken place even five years earlier he could have fled to Hue and opened a new chapter in the contest between Siam and Vietnam, but that option was no longer open. A succession of Vietnamese emperors had been persecuting Catholic converts, and towards the end of

AN AFTERNOON WITH THE SECOND KING

Henri Mouhot's description of an afternoon in the company of Prince Norodom, the 'second king', at Udong in 1859; Norodom was in his early twenties and would become king the following year.

I was introduced by the chamberlain into one of the king's private apartments, a pretty room furnished in the European style. His Majesty sat waiting for me, smoking, near a table covered with refreshments; and as soon as I entered he rose, and holding out his hand, and smiling, he begged me to sit down and begin my repast. I perceived that he intended, after the manner of the country, to do me honour by being present at the meal without partaking of it himself.

After introducing me, with much courtesy and friendliness, to his brother, a young man of fifteen, who was kneeling by his side, the king said, 'I have had this fowl and duck cooked in the European fashion; tell me if they are to your taste.'

All had been really exceedingly well prepared; the fish, particularly, was capital.

'Good brandy,' said the king, in English (the only words he knew in that language), as he pointed to a bottle of cognac. 'Drink,' continued he.

The attendants then placed before me jellies and exquisitely preserved fruits, bananas, and excellent mangoes. Afterwards tea was served, of which the king also partook, having first offered me a Manilla cigar. He then wound up a musical-box, and put it on the table. The first air gave me great pleasure, all the more because I was unprepared

to hear it in a royal palace. It was the Marseillaise. The king took my start and look of astonishment for admiration. 'Do you know that air?' he asked.

'Yes, sire.'

Then followed another scarcely less familiar, the air of the Girondins, Mourir pour la patrie.

'Do you also know that?'

As an answer, I accompanied the air with the words. 'Does your Majesty like this air?' I inquired.

'Not so well as the first.'

'Your Majesty is right; most European sovereigns have the same taste.'

'Napoleon, for instance?'

'Napoleon, particularly.'

My Annamite was with me, and filled the office of interpreter, with a perfect tact which pleased the king. The young prince now asked permission to retire, and saluted his brother by bowing to the earth and raising his clasped hands above his head. The king desired him to return the next morning, and accompany us to the palace of the first king; and the prince, passing out into the courtyard, was lifted astride on the shoulders of an attendant, and carried to his palace.

His Majesty then displayed to me his European furniture, mahogany tables covered with china vases and other ornaments of a commonplace description; above all, he pointed out, as worthy of notice, two old looking-glasses in gilt frames, a sofa, and various similar articles. 'I am but beginning,' said he; 'in a few years my palace will be beautiful.'

August 1858 a French expeditionary force had landed at Da Nang with the ostensible aim of safeguarding the interests of Catholics in the south. This was rather odd, as there were more Catholics in the north, but China fever was infecting the European powers, Paris believed that the unexplored Mekong River represented the back door to the Middle Kingdom, and the delta was in Cochinchina.

The campaign did not go well. The local Catholics failed to rise up against the emperor as they had been expected to do, and while the Vietnamese army was quickly dispersed, the French were met with a tenacious popular resistance. However, they slowly prevailed, and in June 1862 the Emperor Tu Duc agreed to cede Saigon and the three provinces that controlled access to the Mekong. With the addition shortly afterwards of three further provinces, this now became the directly ruled French colony of Cochinchina.

ABOVE
Admiral Lagrandière.

The next step was to secure control of the Cambodian section of the Mekong. In mid-1863, while the Siamese representative at Norodom's court was temporarily absent, Admiral Pierre Paul Marie Benoit de Lagrandière arrived in Udong and offered to protect the king from his enemies, in return for freedom of navigation on the river and control over Cambodia's foreign relations. A French *Résident* would be appointed to the court to oversee France's rights. This, the Admiral said, was no more than a reassertion of the right of suzerainty that France had inherited from the Emperor of Vietnam through its acquisition of Cochinchina.

Norodom signed on 11 August 1863. A succession of historians and writers have claimed that he did so only in response to French bullying (a four-hour deadline with a gunboat on the river outside), but there is little evidence to back this up. Certainly it was not a treaty between equals, and certainly the French were quite willing to apply force to gain their ends, but we should not deny Norodom, that master of indecision and the passive-aggressive mode, his deep desire to escape Siamese domination.

When Norodom's Siamese minders learnt what had happened they were naturally horrified. However, they held a trump card, for Norodom was not yet king, at least not in a ritual sense. No Cambodian monarch could be truly king until he was crowned, and the royal regalia – the crown, the sacred sword and other items – were in the keeping of the Siamese court in Bangkok. The French were no sooner out of sight than Rama IV offered Norodom the chance be crowned, with the proviso that he sign a secret treaty accepting Siam's ownership of Battambang and Siem Reap, and affirming his position as Siam's viceroy in Cambodia. Possibly the Siamese representative convinced Norodom that the French would not be staying in Indochina, and that he would need Bangkok's help to face the wrath of the Emperor of Vietnam when he regained his territories. In any event, the new treaty reduced Norodom from a vassal king to something more like the hereditary governor of a province. It also completely undercut the agreement he had just signed with France, but until he was crowned he would remain vulnerable to challenges from Sivotha, who was still at large, and Sisowath, whose ambitions he distrusted.

Norodom signed the secret treaty on 1 December 1863, and on 3 March 1864 he set out for Kampot to take a ship for Bangkok. On the road a messenger caught up with him, bringing the news that back at Udong French marines had occupied the palace and gunboats were firing a salute to the French flag. There was also a message from the French representative informing him in exquisitely polite language that if he left Cambodia he would never be allowed back. Norodom returned to Udong.

After considerable diplomatic manoeuvring, Paris and Bangkok agreed that Norodom's coronation should proceed in Udong (not Bangkok) and under French auspices. On 3 June 1864, the representative of Rama IV handed the crown to the French representative, who handed it to Norodom, who placed it on his own head. Rama's emissary then read out an address in Thai, which Norodom and probably all the high officials present understood, but which the French did not. He reminded them of Siam's great kindness to Cambodia in the past, of how Cambodia had given the provinces of Battambang and Siem Reap to Siam in gratitude, and of how these territories now belonged to Siam. They were defiant sentiments, but like the secret treaty they had no bearing on the world of hard politics: Cambodia's future lay with France.

THE PROTECTORATE AND ITS DISCONTENTS

And so the French Protectorate began. It soon became apparent that due to the rapids on the Cambodian-Laotian border (the modern border – at this time Siam still controlled the northern provinces), the Mekong River would never be a highway to China, and as Cambodia had little else to offer, Norodom was left to govern his country as he wished. Visitors liked him – 'a pleasant looking ... little man with intelligent and expressive features ... he seduces you from the moment you arrive ... jovial ... vivid spirit, sharp gaze ... a playful and slightly vulgar sense of humour...', – while sneering at his weakness for women and opium, and his vulgar taste in clothes, furniture and hand-me-down palaces. *Notre roitelet* they called him, 'our little kingy'. For the French officials who had to deal with him he was a constant source of frustration, apparently unwilling to take the business of government seriously. 'Without aim and purpose, he pushes ahead but does not wonder where he is going; undecided about everything, of a marvellous duplicity, caprice serves as his only guide.'

Laissez-faire was not to last. France's overseas empire had doubled in size under Napoleon III, but his was a bourgeois empire and barbaric institutions such as slavery and harems were impossible to justify before public opinion. The colonies and possessions contained far too many examples of both, and in 1879 a new governor, Charles le Myre de Vilers, was sent out to Saigon with the explicit mission of reforming Cochinchina. The French language was to be fostered in administration, an elected Colonial Council with a minority of indigenous members was to be established, and a French system of education was to be introduced with the objective in due course of sending talented young Vietnamese to France for their higher studies. The new policy represented, le Myre explained, 'the natural substitution, in some sense fatal, of modern individualism for primitive collectivism. ... [S]uch a state of affairs ... is the inevitable consequence of the development of civilisation'.

Direct intervention was not possible in

*Mixed Cambodian/
French court, 1928. An
independent judiciary
is indispensable to a
functioning democracy.*

nominally independent Cambodia, but an opportunity to exert pressure had arisen in 1877 when Norodom requested French help in putting down an insurrection. The uprising had begun in 1875, triggered by extortionate taxation and the abuses of the *oknha*. Prince Sivotha had placed himself at its head, and the situation had become chronic. The treaty between France and Norodom was meant to have the protection of the king from his enemies at its centre, but now the French withheld their assistance pending his agreement to certain reforms, notably that the French *Résident* would sit with the council of ministers as a 'consultative voice' whenever trade, finances and the legal system were discussed, and beyond that whenever he wished. Slavery was to be abolished in stages, and no new taxes were to be imposed without the council's approval, meaning without the *Résident's* approval.

Norodom agreed and the uprising was put down, although Sivotha escaped. The French felt that they had pulled off a clever piece of politics, but the king, his immediate aim achieved, did all in his power to obstruct the promised reforms. The French expressed disappointment and impatience, and Norodom began searching for ways to protect himself from French bullying. Soon enough the French discovered that he was in secret talks with the Spanish consul in Saigon, which was a direct contravention of the terms of his agreement. Le Myre proposed that he be sent off to Tahiti or Mauritius and replaced with Sisowath, but although Paris agreed that a firmer line was needed, it was decided that he should not be removed.

In 1883, Charles Antoine Francis Thomson, of English ancestors long settled in France, took over from Le Myre. He had before him a memo from his predecessor detailing Norodom's failings. In the north-east the tribal peoples were being hunted and sold as slaves, while in the Khmer heartland the officials went unpaid and lived by pillaging those they were meant to govern. Brigandage was rampant, public services non-existent, roads impassable and bridges in disrepair. The king drew no distinction between public and private revenue, and squandered the nation's taxes on diamonds and other jewels, and the Filipino bands for which he had developed a passion on a visit to Manila. To crown it all there was the royal harem, 'made up of four hundred women, which becomes larger each year through the recruitment of young girls carried on in Siam'.

Nevertheless, while it might seem desirable to remove Norodom, 'the Cambodian is profoundly attached to the monarchic form', and if pressed too hard he could raise the whole country in revolt. A better policy was to encourage Vietnamese colonization. Already this had transformed the provinces of Ha Tien and Chau Doc from Khmer to Vietnamese, and within 50 years they could form the majority of Cambodia's population.

Thomson visited Phnom Penh in June 1884. At his first meeting with Norodom he informed the king that he had a plan of reforms in mind – notably, the expenses of the protectorate would be met by allowing the French to collect the kingdom's customs duties and the taxes on opium and alcohol. Norodom refused to comply. He pointed out that his agreement with France was restricted to protection and foreign relations, and to surrender control over revenue would be an infringement of national sovereignty. Thomson replied that the treaty's promise of protection applied to the kingdom rather than to the king.

The interview ended badly and Norodom, pleading illness, refused to see Thomson again. Early in the morning of 17 June, with three gunboats on the river opposite the royal palace and the streets around blocked off by marines, Thomson and his military aide, a Captain Joseph Jarnowski, entered the king's private apartments without appointment, where Thomson read to him the text of a new agreement. The council of ministers would henceforth be subordinate to the French *Résident-general*, who would have the right of private audience whenever he wished, and French *Résident*s with similar rights would be placed in the provinces. Slavery would be abolished, the right to real property (property in land) would be introduced and the king would accept all future reforms proposed to him. The king's interpreter cried out that this was a demand for abdication, but Norodom had no choice but to sign.

Six months later, at the end of January 1885, the entire country rose in revolt. In March a force of 5,000 rebels almost succeeded in storming Phnom Penh, and by the end of the year French authority was restricted to the main towns and a few police posts. The mobilizing force behind the Great Insurrection seems to have come from local *oknhas*, but it drew in peasants angered at the attack on kingship and the threat of private land ownership, charismatic Buddhist millenarians (believers in the coming end of the world cycle), Chinese merchants threatened by the transfer of financial control to the French, and ordinary bandits. Prince Sivotha once again took charge, and his first target was a French military post near Sambor, leaving no doubt that this was a nationalist rather than a dynastic struggle. He reached out to both Norodom and Sisowath to join him in a war of liberation, but Sisowath demonstrated his loyalty to France by betraying his half-brother's emissaries. The French suspected Norodom of being deeply implicated and they were probably right, since it is hard to see how a coordinated nationwide uprising could have been organized without his knowledge and at least tacit consent, but nothing was ever proved.

The uprising was incredibly brutal on both sides, with summary executions and mass killings, rapes and heads on poles. The insurgents targeted Catholic Vietnamese, while the French were indiscriminate. One of the worst offenders was Captain Jarnowski, stationed in Takeo, who gained a reputation for abducting and raping local women. Reports of his crimes were sent to his superiors in Phnom Penh, but instead of being punished he was nominated for the Legion d'Honneur.

In later years the French would shrug off the insurrection as a minor affair, but in fact they had nearly been thrown out of the country. In July

1886, after 4,000 French troops failed to make an impression on the insurgents, Thomson's successor, Ange Michel Filippini, met with Norodom to offer concessions and ask for the king's assistance in bringing matters to a conclusion. The king issued a proclamation telling his people that Cambodia's sovereignty had been restored to his satisfaction, and by the end of year the rebellion was ended. Sisowath, in the field as leader of the royal army against Sivotha, allowed his half-brother to escape to the jungles of the north-east, where he gradually declined into irrelevance.

Through direct violence, refugee movements and the disruption it caused to normal life, the uprising had caused Cambodia's population to plunge by 20 per cent to three-quarters of a million, proportionately in keeping with the impact of the Khmer Rouge a little less than 100 years later. Nevertheless, it saved Cambodia, for after this the French would be extremely wary of touching Norodom's position. Yet Norodom had not really won at all, because what the French failed to impose at one swoop in 1885, they achieved piecemeal in the following years as Norodom aged and his ministers, once afraid of his anger, became increasingly willing to act against his wishes. The culmination came in 1897, when the council of ministers announced that no royal decision would henceforth have legal force unless it was countersigned by the *Résident-supérieur*. As Norodom's interpreter had feared when Thomson forced the showdown in the palace, the Protectorate had reduced the king to a figurehead.

ABOVE
King Sisowath in coronation dress, wearing the State Crown and holding the royal sword.

HIGH NOON OF EMPIRE

Norodom died in 1904, convinced that his life had ended in failure, but he had preserved the kingdom as best he could. His brother Sisowath had wanted to be king all his life, but unlike Sivotha he was willing to wait, and unlike Sivotha he had his reward. Such brotherly rivalry inside the royal clan had been a constant theme of Cambodian history for centuries. Possibly it can be traced to the practice of the royal harem and the way it encouraged

rivalry among the wives and therefore between their offspring, and perhaps the absence of clear rules for succession played a part, making the throne the property of whoever could gain it and hold it. There is no agreed answer.

The most important event of the new king's reign was Siam's restitution of the long-lost provinces of Battambang, Sisophon and Siem Reap to Cambodia, which is to say, to France, so that by 1907, and for the first time in centuries, most Cambodians were living inside Cambodian frontiers, which were pretty much those of the modern kingdom. A Khmer proverb says '*srok Khmer mun de soun*' (the Khmer land shall never die), and King Sisowath, even though he had nothing to do with events beyond providing the French with a history of how the Siamese had stolen Angkor, regarded this as the crowning achievement of his reign. It was certainly seen as a landmark by Cambodians at the time, although there was some bitterness that France had not agreed to restore the former Cambodian lands in Cochinchina.

By this time France possessed the second largest colonial empire in the world, second only to Britain, and the decade of the 1910s was its high noon. It was the fashion of the time to hold colonial exhibitions to showcase the exotic overseas possessions to the working and middle classes, not least

because there was a considerable groundswell of anti-imperialist sentiment in both Britain and France, and in 1906 the French sent Sisowath and the Royal Ballet to Marseille. Both the king and the Royal Ballet were wildly popular. An entranced Auguste Rodin sketched the crop-headed, rubber-limbed dancers over and over again, while the king charmed the crowds by sending diamond rings to ladies who presented him with bouquets. But he

ABOVE

Tableau on the slope of Wat Phnom, Phnom Penh, commemorating the return of Cambodia's western provinces in 1907.

BELOW

Posters advertising colonial expositions. These expositions were intended to drum up popular support for the overseas empire.

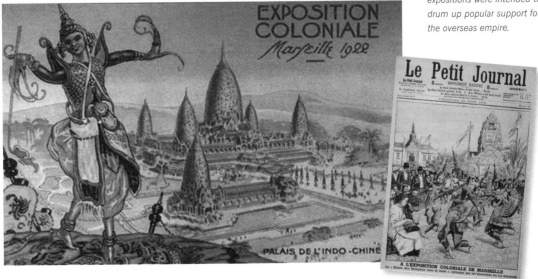

was old, and once back home in Phnom Penh he rarely ventured out of his palace.

The French, who had put Sisowath on the throne, had forgotten the scare of the mid-1880s and considered him a cypher, unimportant to both them and the Cambodian people, but 10 years after the triumphant visit to Marseilles a curious event shook that belief. The First World War was in progress, and revenue collection needed to be rigorously enforced. Perhaps it was a little too rigorously enforced, because in November 1915 a delegation of peasants came to the capital to petition for a reduction in taxes. From their point of view these were the king's taxes and collected by royal officials, so they camped in the square outside the main gate of the royal palace. Sisowath lived in a splendour unknown in Cambodia since Angkor, and they would have been deeply impressed by the gleaming white walls, gold spires and bright tiled roofs among the green of the mango trees. Perhaps they even saw the king's own white elephant, and certainly they would have seen the high officials in their colourful silks, and the French in their solar topees passing through the gates where smartly

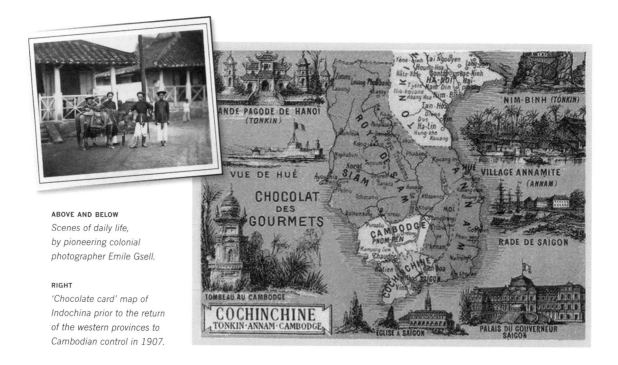

uniformed guards saluted. All this fitted perfectly with their ideas of what a king should be. They were orderly and respectful and perhaps a little over-awed. Sisowath met them and made some vague promises and they went home, satisfied that their lord had heard their grievances.

News of the king's compassion and justice spread, and all through the winter more and more villagers made the pilgrimage to the walls of the palace. Just how many has never been clear, but estimates range from 40,000 to 100,000. Sisowath was as surprised as the French that such numbers could turn out spontaneously to see a king who rarely bothered to make himself visible, but the king in his golden palace, powerless and old, was simultaneously the god Vishnu in the little shrine on the bank of the Mekong River on the far side of the park, whose right eye was Preah Surya, the sun, and whose left eye was Preah Chan, the moon.

To a rational Frenchman this was all superstition – but coinciding with a rising tide of anti-French sentiment in Cochinchina, the situation started to look potentially dangerous. Cambodian villagers paid the highest taxes in all Indochina, on the widest assortment of excuses (taxes on rice, salt, alcohol, opium, charges for every signature on every piece of official paper), and got the least in return. French officials and a tiny Phnom Penh-based elite of royal hangers-on and Sino-Khmer businessmen enjoyed lives of considerable luxury in a beautiful city of tree-lined boulevards that was called the Pearl of Asia, but almost nothing was spent on education and medical services, and electricity and running water were practically unknown outside the capital. French officials never had much contact with Cambodian peasants, and as the years went on they had less and less. The typewriter and the motor car were to blame: the first encouraged headquarters in Phnom Penh to demand more and more reports, which meant more and more time in the office, and the motor car meant that when the *résidents* did go out they visited only places that could be reached by road.

The events over the winter of 1915/16 were not repeated the next year and were forgotten even sooner than the uprising of 1885. It was an error. On 18 April 1925, at about one o'clock in the afternoon, the villagers of Kraang Leav in Kampong Chhnang, a province to the north-west of Phnom

EUROPEAN VISITORS

The years *entre deux guerres* (the period between the two world wars) were the best. In 1908, Jean Commaille, ex-painter, ex-Foreign Legionnaire and first Conservator of Angkor, began living in a grass hut beside the causeway at Angkor Wat. As soon as enough jungle had been cleared to provide snake-free access, with his guidebook in their hands and undeterred by his fate (murdered by bandits in 1916), the visitors came.

They knew about travel in those days. Andre Malraux, foiled in his attempt to hack sculptures from the walls of Banteay Srei, conceived an abiding hatred for the injustices of colonialism and became France's Minister for Culture. Somerset Maugham arrived on the tail end of a tour through Burma, Thailand and Indochina, wrote *The Gentleman in the Parlour* and journeyed on to a rendezvous on a sampan. Charlie Chaplin charmed with his fluent French and left behind the thick black greasepaint moustaches that are still the trademark of Cambodian comics. Norman Lewis, chronicler of mad aunts and author of *A Dragon Apparent*, described Siem Reap as a 'slumbering Shangri-La perfumed slightly with putrid fish-sauce', and hid under the luggage at the back of his bus to avoid bandits. Dennis Bloodworth, veteran correspondent for the *Observer*, was put up as Sihanouk's personal guest solely so that the prince could publicly abuse him on the evening news – he tells of the experience in *An Eye for the Dragon*. Wonder beyond wonders, each one of these visitors very probably found himself alone with the temples for hours at a time.

Penh and bordering the Tonle Sap, murdered Felix Bardez, the *résident* for their province, as he collected unpaid tax on paddy (newly harvested rice). Until 1920 this had been collected by royal officials, and the traditional procedure was that the officials sat down with the village elders and asked how much paddy had been harvested, the elders named a figure that both sides knew to be untrue, and after some discussion a compromise would be reached. This had been the way for centuries, and the only real change after the French took charge was that the officials were now sent out by provincial *résidents*.

Bardez's death was entirely his own fault, in that *résidents* did not normally go out personally to collect taxes. Bardez did, because he was conscientious, unimaginative and determined to please his superiors. In his previous posting in Prey Veng province his diligence had brought about a marked rise in revenue, catching the attention of *Résident-supérieur* François-Marius Baudoin. Baudoin had committed himself to an extensive programme of public works, and especially roads, since this was the age of the automobile and the French Empire was nothing if not modern. Between 1900 and 1930, 9,000km (5,592 miles) of roads, paved and unpaved, were built using corvée labour, as Jayavarman VII had built his. One does not wish to press the parallels with Angkor too far, but also like Jayavarman, Baudoin went in for monument building, in his case not temples but an ambitious resort complex on top of Bokor Mountain near Kampot. This was dubbed 'Baudoin's Folly' by the anti-colonialist press in Saigon and Hanoi, and was reputed to have cost 900 lives. Roads and resorts, not to mention the new *palais de justice* in Phnom Penh and a new yacht as a gift for King Sisowath, were expensive, and Baudoin may have pressed Bardez to repeat his success in Prey Veng in his new province.

Bardez arrived in Kraang Laev at eight in the morning, accompanied by a single militiaman and an interpreter. The villagers sat on the ground outside the *sala* (open-sided meeting hall) beside the village monastery and the elders sat inside. Through his interpreter, Bardez reminded them of their obligations and asked them to pay what was owed. As this produced no result he pointed out three elders at random and ordered the militiaman to tie them up. They would not be released, he said, until the tax was paid. They could think about this while he had lunch.

While he was away the wife of one of the men borrowed the money owed by her husband, a little over five dollars, and when Bardez returned she asked for him to be released as she wanted to take him home. There are differing accounts of what happened next, but it is most likely that Bardez told the woman that nobody would be released until all the back taxes were paid. Another man, not one of those tied up, told the woman to take her husband anyway. The woman touched her husband on the arm and the militiaman pointed his rifle and cocked it, 'so we pushed the rifle away and punched him'. In the melée that followed, the militiaman, Bardez and the interpreter were beaten to death.

Eighteen suspects (a nineteenth died during questioning) were put on trial in December 1925. What was at issue was not their guilt but the nature of their crime. Baudoin's enemies, and he had many, painted the incident as a *jacquerie*, a peasant uprising sparked by oppressive taxation and therefore a sign and result of colonial oppression. The view of the colonial authorities was that the death of Bardez had had no political implications but was a simple and meaningless murder.

If official France was determined to see in the Bardez case no more than an outbreak of criminality, it was because it was terrified of what it might mean if it were not. The retrocession of Battambang in 1907 should have endeared the French to the Khmers of the province, but instead it had been followed by two years of insurrection. It was true that the uprising had been feudal, not anti-colonial, in character, but the leaders had shown an uncomfortable willingness to name France as the alien occupier of the Khmer lands. The high noon of empire had passed, and a new nationalism was at work in the colonial East.

THE BIRTH OF THE MODERN

During 1914–1918, 2,000 ordinary Cambodians had gone to Europe to fight and to serve in labour battalions, but the Cambodian response to French recruitment campaigns had been far from overwhelming – in fact it had bordered on the hostile. They had now returned, potentially infected with dangerous ideas about socialism and democracy. Nationalism was well advanced in Vietnam, a revolution in China had demonstrated that attachment to tradition might not be as strong as hoped (and a source of clear but unpredictable danger when one-third of the population of Phnom Penh was Chinese), and in India the British were facing down increasingly strident

BELOW

Tourist posters of the early 20th century advertising Angkor.

calls for drastic reform. Then there was rising Japan, showing what Asians could do without Europeans. Cambodia was almost miraculously quiet, but official France was uneasy.

Cambodia was slow in developing a modern anti-colonialist movement, and the reason probably lies in the nature and reach of education. In India and Vietnam the beneficiaries of Western education had been the first to agitate for greater independence. Liberal administrators in the British empire realized the wisdom of going at least halfway to meet legitimate aspirations, but their conservative colleagues took away the lesson that education was a bad idea. The prejudice had a very long history: in 1792 a director of the East India Company gave his opinion that America was lost because Britain established schools there, and 'it would not do for us to repeat the same act of folly in India'. 'Educated Vietnamese', declared the *Résident-supérieur* of Tonkin (northern Vietnam), '[are] revolutionaries and malcontents, detached from their culture, the rice field, and the artisan's shop', and a danger to themselves and their superiors.

In Cambodia there was no such threat. The pagoda schools opposed French efforts to introduce a modern curriculum, and only feeble moves were made to set up a handful of modern Western-style schools in the inter-war years. This meant that Cambodia remained insulated from Vietnamese-style nationalism, but the failure to educate Cambodians to a level where they could play a role in the administration, even assuming the French would have welcomed such a development, meant that the lower levels

were staffed by Vietnamese. The average villager interacting with the Protectorate met not a Frenchman but a Vietnamese clerk, who almost invariably treated him with contempt and required a bribe to put his seal on whatever piece of paper was required.

To counter the possibility of Vietnamese-style nationalism, the French fostered a sense of Cambodian nationhood, focused backwards on a glorious and safely distant past that would tie the Khmers to their history and divide them from the Vietnamese. The conservation and promotion of Angkor was the primary avenue for this, but equally important was the Buddhist Institute of Phnom Penh, set up in 1931 under the direction of the Buddhist scholar Suzanne Karpelès, and its journal *Kampuchea Surya* ('Cambodian Sun'), in which young Cambodian intellectuals could publish learned articles on aspects of Cambodian culture alongside new fiction and poetry. In 1936 two members of this circle, Son Ngoc Thanh and Pach Chhoeun, both from Kampuchea Krom, launched Cambodia's first Khmer-language newspaper, *Nagaravatta* (Angkor Wat). The publication was not anti-French, but rather drew attention to the administration's favouritism towards Vietnamese and the lack of employment opportunities for educated Khmers. *Nagaravatta* was the first tentative step towards a modern Cambodian nationalism, but its circulation was tiny and it had almost no impact on society at large. The Second World War was destined to change everything.

ABOVE
Nagaravatta, the first Khmer-language newspaper.

BELOW
The seal of the Buddhist Institute. This and the newspaper were important influences in the formation of modern Cambodian nationalism.

SECOND WAR AND FIRST INDEPENDENCE

War broke out in Europe in September 1939, but it was not until mid-1940 that fighting began on the Western front. When it did Paris fell within weeks and France surrendered. A new and neutral government was formed at Vichy, but Charles de Gaulle escaped to England, where he formed the Free French and vowed to fight on: '*La France a perdu une bataille, mais la France n'a pas perdu la guerre!*' ('France has lost a battle, but France has not lost the war'). However, with the French army now in German prison camps and her navy confined to harbour, neutrality was more a necessity than a policy, and the overseas possessions would have to look after themselves.

In the Orient the dominant military power was not Germany but Japan, which was at war with China. The Chinese were importing arms and fuel from Haiphong through Hanoi in Vietnam to Yunnan, and the Japanese were determined to stop them. A brief war from 22 to 26 September 1940 resulted in French defeat, and Admiral Jean Decoux, Vichy's Governor-General of Indochina, was forced to give Tokyo the right to station troops throughout the colonies. This eventually included a garrison of 8,000 in Phnom Penh.

It was against this background that Prince Norodom Sihanouk became king. When he was born, on 31 October 1922, Phnom Penh was a charming town of canals and tree-lined boulevards stretching along the banks of the Mekong and Tonle Sap Rivers, with a French quarter in the north, a Chinese quarter in the middle and a Cambodian quarter around the palace in the south. The three populations had little to do with each other: the Khmer were functionaries and palace hangers-on, the Chinese and Sino-Khmer ran commerce, and the French ran the country. King Sisowath, Sihanouk's great-grandfather, had died in 1927 and had been succeeded by his son, Monivong, amid rumours of a large bribe paid to *Résident-supérieur* Boudoin. Monivong proved an indolent monarch, and Sihanouk later recalled watching him reclining in a hammock as he signed documents without bothering to read them. For the French he was an ideal *roitelet*.

Sihanouk was at school in Saigon in mid-November 1940 when Thailand (the name had recently changed from the traditional Siam) took advantage of France's weakness and its own friendship with Japan to occupy border areas of Cambodia. The French were momentarily distracted by an uprising of the Indochinese Communist Party in Cochinchina, but on 16 January 1941 they counter-attacked. The Thais claimed victory in the resulting battle but it was more accurately a draw, with both sides withdrawing from the area. The next day the French scored an undeniable victory when they took the Thai navy by surprise at Koh Chang and sank several ships. Japan, concerned that an Asian nation should not suffer defeat at the hands of a discredited European colonialist power, stepped in to force an end to the fighting. France was obliged to restore the northern and western provinces of Cambodia to Thai control, although Cambodia was permitted to retain Angkor. Monivong, who had been unwaveringly pro-French throughout his life, retired to his villa at Bokor, where for the few remaining months of his life he refused to receive French officials or to hear French spoken in his presence.

Monivong died in April 1941. Admiral Decoux now had to find a successor from the large royal clan, divided by rivalry between its Norodom and Sisowath branches. One candidate was Prince Sisowath Monireth, Monivong's eldest son, who had once told the founders of *Nagaravatta* that education was a waste of time and would only make people difficult to govern. Also mentioned was Prince Sisowath Sirik Matak, who was hard-working and honest but condescending and aloof. Or there was Prince Norodom Suramarit, easy-going and liberal minded, who had accepted the position of patron of *Nagaravatta* after Monireth turned it down.

The choice was none of these but the teenage Norodom Sihanouk, Suramarit's son. The French insisted that they had chosen him because his double descent from the Sisowath and Norodom families would heal the feud between them. This may have been part of the reasoning, but more probable is that Sihanouk, young, malleable and uninterested in politics, looked like a *roitelet*. 'They thought I was a lamb,' he was to remark many years later. 'They found I was a tiger.'

Sihanouk was crowned on 3 May 1941, in the middle of dangerous times. Nationalism was on the rise in Vietnam and even in Cambodia, and politically aware Khmers were beginning to ask what would happen after Japan won the war. Decoux and his officials also felt sure that Japan would win, but they were determined that after it did, Cambodia and Indochina would remain in the French orbit.

Nagaravatta had a different opinion. The newspaper was now becoming increasingly anti-French, and although its readership was tiny it was one that mattered, the first rudimentary core of an educated urban middle class owing nothing to royal patronage. The French redoubled their championing of tradition as a vaccine against nationalism. Sihanouk, descendant and living incarnation of the great Jayavarman VII, was encouraged to travel throughout the kingdom. No king had ever been seen like this, and everywhere he went there were adoring crowds. Sihanouk, at first shy and uncertain of his role, began to enjoy himself, and discovered a talent for oratory.

In July 1942, two monks were arrested for preaching anti-French sermons to the militia. The arrests could probably have passed without comment beyond nationalist circles, but the fact that the two were taken into

ABOVE
Monivong.

BELOW
Sihanouk in his coronation regalia, November 1941.

custody without being allowed to disrobe turned the incident into a public outrage. Pach Chhoeun, using *Nagaravatta* as his platform, organized a massive march to the *Résidence Supérieure*, where furniture was smashed and officials assaulted. He had counted on Japanese support, but none was forthcoming, and he was arrested and exiled to the prison island of Poulo Condore (now Con Son), while his colleague Son Ngoc Thanh fled to Bangkok and eventually to Tokyo. *Nagaravatta* was closed down.

With most militant nationalists in jail or in Japan, the French proceeded to implement two administrative reforms that had been under development for some time. Official documents henceforth were to be in a Romanized version of Khmer, and the European calendar was to replace the Cambodian one for official purposes. To the French these seemed minor matters, and entirely logical – why should Cambodia not use more rational ways of writing and more modern ways of telling time? For the Cambodians they were an attack on Khmer civilization. Sihanouk protested on behalf of all Khmers, but to no avail.

By the end of 1942, the world had seen German advances turn into retreats at Alamein and Stalingrad, Operation Torch had brought the Americans to North Africa, and Japan had been defeated at Midway and Guadalcanal. It began to become evident to clear-sighted observers that Japan and Germany were going to lose the war after all, and Decoux put out feelers to de Gaulle. In June 1944 the Allies landed in France, and by August–September de Gaulle was in command in Paris. By early 1945 the British were advancing rapidly through Burma and the Americans in the Philippines, and French anti-aircraft batteries in Indochina were refusing to fire on American bombers targeting the docks at Haiphong and Saigon. Even Phnom Penh came under attack, a raid on Phnom Penh on 7 February hitting Wat Unalom by mistake and killing a number of monks and civilians. On 9 March the Japanese removed the French administration and interned most French military and administrative personnel. On 12 March, at Japan's invitation, Sihanouk voided all agreements with France, overturned the hated decrees on language and the calendar, and proclaimed the independence of the Kingdom of Kampuchea.

At Sihanouk's request the Japanese brought Son Ngoc Thanh back to Phnom Penh to serve as foreign minister. Thanh had by now become an anti-monarchist fascist, and on 6 August he held a massive march-past of

30,000 supporters outside the royal palace, a third of Phnom Penh's 100,000 population. On 9 August a group of young hotheads broke into the palace, demanding the abdication of Sihanouk and the appointment of a new government headed by Thanh, while students rallied a block away in the grounds of Lycée Sisowath. Thanh was not behind this event and he and Prince Monireth combined to defuse the situation, but when Japan surrendered on 15 August 1945 Sihanouk promoted him to prime minister.

Between 15 August and 8 October, when a force of British Gurkhas arrived to take the Japanese surrender in Phnom Penh, Thanh had managed to alienate everyone. The British were careful to do nothing of a political nature, and on 15 October General Jacques-Philippe Leclerc de Hauteclocque, liberator of Paris and newly appointed Commander of the French Far East Expeditionary Corps, arrived from Saigon. Thanh entered the room as prime minister expecting to negotiate Cambodia's independence, but Leclerc arrested him and flew him back to Saigon the same day, from where he was eventually sent into exile in France. Pach Chhoeun and other nationalists fled to the border, where they took up armed resistance with Thai support under the name Khmer Issarak ('Free Khmers').

A ROYAL CRUSADE

With Thanh removed Monireth resumed the prime ministership, and on 4 January 1946 it was agreed that Cambodia would henceforth be an independent kingdom within the Indochinese Federation, itself a component of the newly created French Union. Both Federation and Union were intended to meet American objections to the existence of colonial empires, but there was no doubt that the intention was to keep Indochina French.

The Protectorate was formally at an end, but France retained control of foreign relations, with the result that Cambodia could not join the United Nations or exchange embassies with other countries. France also controlled its defence and military affairs, so that operations against the Khmer Issarak were conducted by forces under French command. A system of parallel administration meant that French officials continued to supervise everything from revenue to telegraphs and railways. The Issarak were understandably dismissive of this threadbare independence, and for a week in August, 300 of their fighters occupied Siem Reap before being driven back. The attack leader, Dap Chhuon, would play an important role in later political events.

As a result of American pressure, the January 1946 agreement included provision for a democratically elected Constitutional assembly that would draw up a constitution for a democratic Cambodia. Sihanouk, possibly under the inspiration of his liberal father, Prince Suramarit, insisted that the elections be held under conditions of freedom of speech and of association, so that for the first time in Cambodia's history political parties could be formed. Two significant parties contested the vote, the Liberals and the Democrats. The former, despite their name, were deeply conservative, advocating cautious and gradual progress towards democracy and a continuing close relationship with France. They drew their support from royalists and the Sino-Khmer business class, and their finance, covertly, from the French. Their opponents, the Democratic Party, were led by Prince Sisowath Youthevong, a French-educated aristocrat with a genuine commitment to parliamentary democracy and an understanding of what an open society meant. His followers were teachers, civil servants and politically active members of the Buddhist monkhood. The Democrats, the only party with a grass-roots organization, won 50 of the 67 seats, and the Democrat-dominated Assembly drew up a constitution with legislative power vested in an elected National Assembly, while the king served as Head of State.

The elections for the National Assembly were held on 1 September, the Democrats won 50 of the 67 seats, and Prince Youthvong became prime minister of a government committed to a programme of anti-colonialism and modernization. Cambodia's experiment with democracy had begun well, but Youthevong died unexpectedly in mid-1947, and without a leader of his calibre and, one might add, without a broad and educated middle class such as the British had created in India, events quickly went downhill.

The Constitution itself was problematic, based as it was on that of the French Fourth Republic. Like the Fourth Republic, democratic Cambodia saw a succession of short-lived governments brought down one after another by a divided Assembly while problems mounted, chief among them the threat posed by Issarak insurgents in the countryside.

Democracy in its infancy was giving itself a bad name. 'I have never been one of those *roitelets*', Sihanouk was later to say, but thus far he had devoted his time largely to the usual pursuits of playboy monarchs and left the business of government to others, such as Monireth. In September 1949, for the first time but not the last, he intervened decisively, dismissing the bickering

Assembly and announcing that elections would be postponed indefinitely. For the next two years, Cambodia was ruled by ministries appointed by the king. This produced stability in government, but had the unfortunate result that those who opposed the king, both Issarak and Democrats, were able to claim that he was a lackey of the French.

After almost two years of royal rule, demands for elections were mounting, and Sihanouk asked the French to bring Son Ngoc Thanh back from exile. His motives have never been satisfactorily explained: the initiative may have come from his father, who had long been a close friend of Thanh's, or perhaps Sihanouk thought that Thanh's ambitions would further split the Democrats. Sihanouk, who prided himself on his popularity, must have been disconcerted when a crowd of half a million turned out to greet Thanh's arrival on 29 October 1951, but in March 1952 his rival fled to the Thai border, where he joined the Issarak and called for the overthrow of the monarchy. Sihanouk, suspecting that the Democrats intended to combine with the Issarak and their communist Viet Minh allies in Vietnam, and aware also that he needed to counter the appeal of their claims to represent Khmer nationalism, dissolved the National Assembly and announced that Cambodia would be given full independence within three years.

The French ignored him and the Issarak denounced him as a colonialist stooge. Early in 1953 he left for France, ostensibly for his health, but once there he wrote to President Auriol to warn that popular support for France was rapidly evaporating. Since 1949, the Democrats had demonstrated that they were incapable of governing, and the Issarak and Viet Minh were gaining strength daily. Genuine independence was the only thing that could prevent the country from falling to communism, but the French government, unconvinced, hinted that the king was not indispensable and might be replaced.

Sihanouk travelled onwards to put his case in Washington. Vice-president Richard Nixon, while not unsympathetic to the king's desire for independence, found him totally unrealistic regarding the wider global

BELOW
Richard Nixon announces the limited ground invasion of Cambodia on national television, 20 April 1970.

struggle. Cambodia lacked the military strength to defeat the communists, and it was therefore in Sihanouk's best interest to keep the French connection. Thwarted at the official level, Sihanouk gave an interview to the *New York Times* in which he expressed his fear that if real independence were not granted in the very near future, the Cambodian people and army would rebel and join the Viet Minh. It was the first of many occasions on which he would go over the heads of his interlocutors and use the media to his advantage.

He returned to Phnom Penh on 17 May to a huge public rally, at which he racked up the emotional tension even further. It was to be independence or nothing. Two weeks later he crossed uninvited into Thailand, and announced that he would not return to Cambodia until full independence was achieved. The French were now convinced that Sihanouk was planning open rebellion – he had 'run amok', General de Langlade, the French commander in Indochina, told the US ambassador in Saigon. They and the Americans discussed replacing him with a more amenable king, but had to reject the idea as too dangerous given Sihanouk's popularity.

Made unwelcome in Bangkok, which was now firmly pro-American and anti-communist, Sihanouk moved back into Cambodia and took up residence in his royal villa next to the ruins of Angkor. This was the headquarters of the Issarak warlord Dap Chhuon, who had come over to the government and been awarded Siem Reap and the western provinces as a semi-autonomous personal fief. Chhuon retained command over his troops and Sihanouk, with his charisma, could call up tens or hundreds of thousands of volunteers. He began doing exactly that, making passionate speeches over the radio calling on the Khmers to demand freedom, and huge mass rallies disturbed the peace of Phnom Penh.

General de Langlade capitulated. As he wrote to Paris, the fight against the Viet Minh in Vietnam was going badly, public support for it in France was rapidly collapsing and putting down a mass insurrection in Cambodia would require at least 15 battalions, which was far more than France could command. Independence, on the other hand, would guarantee Cambodia's support in the fight against the Viet Minh, and safeguard France's economic and cultural legacy. Sihanouk returned to Phnom Penh in triumph to celebrate Cambodia's first Independence Day on 9 November 1953.

THE SANGKUM ERA

For the next quarter of a century Sihanouk was Cambodia. He was a paradox and a spectacle, ebulliently sociable yet capable of a spine-freezing '*Altesse!*' if his dignity were infringed, a dictator who presided over public audiences at which peasants were free to accuse ministers of graft, a tightrope walker between East and West who kept his country out of war for decades. The world has rarely seen so colourful and talented a ruler, or one so fatally flawed.

For now, with independence in his hands, he was supreme. The Democrats were in disarray and the communists and Issarak, although they operated throughout half the country, were capable only of minor attacks. Sihanouk was convinced, not unreasonably, that he was indispensable, 'the natural ruler of the country', as he told a French journalist.

France's long war in Vietnam ended the next year in defeat, and

Cambodia participated in the peace talks in Geneva from April through July 1954. Through adroit diplomacy, Sihanouk's delegation managed to exclude Cambodia's communists from the table (the Cambodian communists regarded their abandonment by Vietnam as a betrayal, a fact that would create lasting distrust of Hanoi), and to avoid the creation of a safe haven for them inside the country. The conference concluded with ceasefire agreements for all parties and a Cambodian complaint about the failure to discuss the border with Vietnam, which was fixed unilaterally by France.

The Geneva Accords, as the agreement was called, stipulated that elections for governments representing the wills of the Vietnamese, Laotian and Cambodian people were to be held by the end of 1955. The Democrats, despite the slow erosion of their popularity, remained the best-organized party and were expected to put in a strong result even if they failed to win outright. To their left was Krom Prachaechon, the 'People's Group', essentially the legal front of the Cambodian communists, for although the communists and the Pracheachon were nominally separate organizations, key individuals, including Saloth Sar, later to adopt the name Pol Pot, worked to coordinate their policies and tactics. Both the Democrats and Pracheachon ran on platforms of anti-monarchism, non-alignment and socialism. They were popular with younger educated Khmers, but feared and disliked by conservatives, the business community and Sihanouk, who had no intention of letting them form a government. Far better, he felt, to rule himself.

His problem was that the Constitution prohibited his direct involvement in politics. He launched his first attempt to get around this in February 1955 with a referendum on the question of whether he had delivered on his promise of independence. At the polling booths police presented voters with two cards, one white and one black, the white card bearing the king's face and the black card the word 'NO'. The instruction was to tear up one card on the spot. Not surprisingly, the referendum returned a resounding endorsement of Sihanouk. Afterwards, the diplomatic corps and members of International Control Commission (the body charged with monitoring the forthcoming election) were summoned to a royal audience, where Sihanouk announced that he intended to ban political parties and appoint ministers himself. The referendum, he explained, had demonstrated that '[t]he Cambodian spirit ... associate[s] the government with the king'.

Sihanouk was surprised and dismayed to find that France, the US and other Western nations opposed the idea – surprised because he had not expected opposition, dismayed because his budget relied on Western aid. The military part of the budget in particular was already a problem, as the French had let it be known that due to ongoing operations in Algeria they could not afford to carry on supporting Cambodia. His new solution, which he put into effect on 2 March, was to abdicate. If the Constitution prohibed the king from engaging in politics, he would not be king. His father became King Suramarit, while King Sihanouk was now Prince Sihanouk, private citizen.

Throughout his life Sihanouk was a brilliant tactician and a dreadful strategist, and at this point he seems to have had no long-term plan. But the elections were to be held in September and he intended to beat the Democrats and Pracheachon at their own game. To do this it would be necessary to steal their clothes. Non-alignment was a major plank in the platform of his opponents, and while waiting for the elections he visited India, where prime minister Jawaharlal Nehru was the world's foremost apostle of non-alignment. The meeting went extremely well, and in a private letter to his sister Nehru described Sihanouk as a 'bright young man with vague ideas', desirous of doing good but lacking adequate advisors and under intense pressure from the Americans to bring Cambodia into the global war on communism.

From India, Sihanouk went to Indonesia to attend the Bandung Conference, where he formally joined Cambodia to the non-aligned bloc and struck up a warm friendship with Chinese foreign minister Zhou Enlai. Personal relationships such as this and the equally warm relationship with Charles de Gaulle seem to have been behind a great deal of Sihanouk's foreign policy, and no doubt his domestic policy, but he was not naive: asked shortly afterwards by a senior British diplomat (Malcolm MacDonald, son of Ramsay MacDonald, Britain's first Labour prime minister) whether he trusted Chinese and North Vietnamese assurances that they would never dream of interfering in Cambodia's domestic affairs, he laughed.

On his return to Phnom Penh, Sihanouk formed his own political front, the Sangkum Reastr Niyum, or 'People's Socialist Community'. The Liberals and other conservative parties voted to fold themselves into the new organization, and all government servants were required to join, a move that gave Sangkum an instant organizational base down to village level to match the Democrats. Still afraid that the Democrats held a reasonable chance of winning, he appointed his friend, Dap Chhuon, infamous for his brutality at Siem Reap, as Director of National Security in charge of all police. The US ambassador reported to Washington that the elections were held in an atmosphere of 'cold, intangible terror', Sangkum took a clean sweep of seats, and India, Poland and Canada, as international observers charged with monitoring them and for reasons that had more to do with diplomacy than with electoral reality, certified that Cambodia had completed its obligations under the Geneva Accords.

Cambodia was now a de facto one-party state. Any public servant who wished for advancement would be well advised to join the Sangkum, and any businessman who wanted a government contract had no option but to donate to it. In August 1957, the Democrats voted to dissolve after their leaders were subjected to a three-hour public harangue from the prince followed by a bashing by the palace guard, and with them went the last forlorn hope that Cambodia might become a genuine democracy. There were polls again in 1958, the last in which Pracheachon candidates came forward, and in 1962 and 1966, but they were a travesty of democracy.

SIHANOUK SURROUNDED

Before the 1955 elections, Sihanouk had signed an agreement on military aid (training, provision of equipment and support for military salaries) with the United States. It was one element in a foreign policy of balanced non-alignment, and balance was everywhere. The United States built a highway from Phnom Penh to Sihanoukville, and the Soviet Union donated a modern hospital to the capital. China was also generous, and in July 1958 Sihanouk extended diplomatic recognition to Beijing. This appalled the United States, for which the isolation of communist China was a key foreign policy aim. It also angered Thailand and South Vietnam, both firmly in the American camp. Phnom Penh and Bangkok were already in dispute over the revered border temple of Preah Vihear, and in November, faced with stalemated negotiations, Sihanouk abruptly broke off diplomatic relations. Leading figures in the Bangkok junta considered bombing Cambodia to bring the prince to his senses, and Washington was willing to give serious consideration to regime change, but the US ambassador, echoing what generations of French officials had told Paris, advised his superiors that 'no government established in Cambodia as [a] result [of] Thai or other outside intervention would be able to govern [the] country'.

The worsening relationship with Vietnam, Thailand and the United States entangled itself with domestic Cambodian politics and person-alities to produce what came to be known as the Bangkok Plot of 1959. One of the central figures in this event was Sam Sary, a long-time ally of Sihanouk who had played a central role in the negotiations at Geneva in 1954 before becom-ing the prince's right-hand man in the Sangkum. The Americans regarded him as their staunchest friend in Cambodia, but Kem Vannsak, a leading Democrat politician, described him as 'a bestial man [who] handed out arms and money to hired ruffians to come and break up our meetings'. In 1958 he was appointed ambassador to the United Kingdom to take him away from a cor-

ABOVE
Sam Sary in London.

ruption scandal, but once in London he created a new and worse scandal by beating his children's governess so badly that she had to be hospitalized. Sam told the London press that he could not understand the fuss, as thrashing one's servants was quite normal in Cambodia. Recalled to Phnom Penh in disgrace, he had a bitter falling out with Sihanouk and fled to Saigon, where he offered a plan to depose the prince with the help of the Thai and South Vietnamese governments, and Son Ngoc Thanh and Dap Chhuon.

Dap Chhuon was by now disenchanted with Sihanouk who, he felt, had shown himself dangerously soft on communism. Skeletally thin, his un-blinking eyes set deep in his skull, his gaze unwavering, he was feared and respected as an adept of black magic, invulnerable to bullets and knives, scrupulously honest and a lifelong anti-communist. In 1956 he had written a confidential letter to the US ambassador in Phnom Penh expressing his willingness to use 'forceful measures' to frustrate Sihanouk's neutralism, but Washington, while essentially in favour of removing Sihanouk, had decided that it was not politically feasible to do so. As for Son Ngoc Thanh, he was now at the head of the Khmer Serei ('White Khmers'), the successors of the

Issarak, with guerrilla forces on the Thai and South Vietnamese borders.

In January 1959 the plotters met in Bangkok. They agreed that Chhuon in Siem Reap would use his three battalions to seal off the Western provinces and declare an autonomous zone, while Son Ngoc Thanh would carry out guerrilla operations throughout the country. The Thais and South Vietnamese would move troops to the borders, and if Sihanouk did not see reason and appoint Thanh to head a pro-Western government, he would be overthrown.

The plot-makers' security was appalling, and the intelligence services of France, the Soviet Union and China immediately informed Sihanouk of what was afoot. Sam Sary and Son Ngoc Thanh were out of Sihanouk's reach, but Dap Chhuon was captured and shot in Siem Reap, and posters of his bloodied body were nailed on the streets of Phnom Penh. In his villa were 270 kilos of gold bullion, plus a radio transmitter in the care of two Vietnamese technicians and an attaché from the US embassy named Victor Matsui. The Americans later explained that Matsui had merely been keeping the embassy informed of the governor's intentions. They did not explain why the embassy had not informed Sihanouk of this, or why Washington had not joined Paris, Moscow and Beijing in warning him of the plot.

A coda occurred on 31 August when a suitcase bomb blew up inside the royal palace. It was obviously meant for Sihanouk, but killed the Chief of Protocol instead. Sam Sary, Son Ngoc Thanh and the Americans were all suspected, but responsibility probably rested with South Vietnamese strongman Ngo Dinh Diem. In any event, the incident confirmed in Sihanouk's mind that he was surrounded by enemies.

HEAD OF STATE

In September 1960, the Third National Congress of the Vietnamese Workers Party, meeting in Hanoi, decided on measures to revive the revolutionary struggle in the south with the aim of reuniting Vietnam. Arms and men were to be sent from the north to the south, and to this end the eastern provinces of Laos and Cambodia were to be developed as a supply route.

Cambodia's communists at this point were in disarray, subject to arrest, torture and extrajudicial execution by Sihanouk's secret police. Above-ground leftists were in no better position, their newspapers operating at Sihanouk's whim and their lives and liberty no safer than those of their underground brethren. In this atmosphere, on 30 September 1960, a secret meeting of Cambodian leftists took place in an abandoned railway carriage at the Phnom Penh train station. There the party changed its name from Kampuchean People's Revolutionary Party to Khmer Workers Party, signalling that Cambodia's communists no longer regarded themselves as the little brothers of the Vietnamese; and Solath Sar (Pol Pot) was elevated to the number three position in the central committee.

King Suramarit died in the same year and Sihanouk promoted himself, via another bogus referendum, to the position of Head of State, an extra-Constitutional dictator untrammelled even by the traditional constraints of kingship. The next three years were the high summer of his rule. The economy was in good shape, and with his coffers filled by the government monopoly on the sale of rice, Sihanouk created government jobs for the urban middle class, beautified the capital with monuments and public buildings, and descended on villages by motorcade and helicopter to inaugurate schools, dams, parks, factories and hospitals, and deliver speeches that went on for hours. He implemented what he called Buddhist socialism, the socialism practised at Angkor, where the common people loved their kings because their kings were the source of justice and prosperity. Buddhist socialism, he explained to Mao, meant that the rich gave their money voluntarily to the poor. 'Socialism is very complicated,' murmured Mao.

Meanwhile the war in Vietnam was intensifying, North Vietnam stepped up the traffic on the Ho Chi Minh Trail, and the Americans and South Vietnamese alternately pleaded and hectored Sihanouk to do something about it. He did nothing, so Washington and Saigon launched incursions that inevitably harmed Cambodian villagers. In November 1963, shortly after Ngo Dinh Diem was assassinated in a coup widely believed to have been instigated by the US embassy and the CIA, Sihanouk cut off all US aid in Cambodia, both civilian and military. Diplomatic relations were broken off entirely in May 1965, following repeated American bombing of Cambodian villages and the appearance of an article in *Newsweek* magazine accusing the prince's mother, Queen Kossamak, of running a string of brothels.

At the same time as quarrelling with the Americans, the prince opened Sihanoukville port to Chinese and Soviet military shipments. The arrangement was meant to be secret, but the resulting increase in the flow of North Vietnamese infiltrating the South could hardly be hidden. This further infuriated the Americans, who now had 200,000 troops in South Vietnam (the number would rise to half a million by 1967), but for Sihanouk it meant that Cambodia's own communists were outflanked, advised now by Hanoi to cooperate with Sihanouk for the greater good. 'When we become pro-American,' Sihanouk explained to a journalist, 'the Chinese and Vietnamese immediately become our enemies ... [F]or this reason I think that we have greater advantages in continuing to quarrel with the Americans.'

THE SHADOWS LENGTHEN

In 1966, General de Gaulle, now president of France, paid a visit to Cambodia. Sihanouk idolized de Gaulle and concentrated all his efforts on making the event a success, with motorcades through the schoolchildren-lined avenues of the capital, a massive public rally at Vann Molyvann's Olympic Stadium (10,000 people turned out to hear de Gaulle speak), and a performance by the Royal Ballet on the terraces of Angkor Wat. Security was tight – Sihanouk warned that the enemy in Thailand would attempt to assassinate the visitor – but foreign media coverage was extensive and positive, and de Gaulle praised his host's wisdom in keeping Cambodia out of America's Asian wars. It was a great success in terms of boosting Sihanouk's stature, and a milestone for international recognition of Cambodia's principled foreign policy, but he had taken his eye off the ball, for he had not given close supervision to preparations for the elections that were taking place soon after. The resulting Assembly was the first since 1955 whose members were not handpicked by Sihanouk, and therefore not inherently loyal to him.

In any case, Sihanouk's rule was facing problems in every direction. The end of American military aid had cut into the efficiency of the armed forces and the incomes of military officers,

BELOW
Charles de Gaulle in Cambodia.

and the end of civilian aid had alienated the Sino-Khmer commercial elite (and Sihanouk had compounded the harm by nationalizing the banks and the export-import trade). Out in the villages the farmers continued to pay high taxes for little or no benefit, as they had done for centuries, and in the capital the creation of jobs could not keep up with the exponentially increasing pool of high-school and university graduates. Wages were stagnant, middle-class living standards were falling, and leftist teachers and professors were alerting their students to causes and remedies.

The economy was falling into ruin. From an average growth rate of 2.5 per cent a year in 1959 and 1963, gross national income had turned negative after 1965. Without an abundant stream of money the politics of patronage became increasingly difficult, and Sihanouk's previous deft touch deserted him. In 1965, faced with a growing hole in the state budget, he nationalized the export-import trade, and Cambodia's businessmen, frozen out of legitimate commerce, turned to the black market. Specifically they turned to the rice trade. This was supposedly a state monopoly and the single largest source of state funds, but soon a quarter of the crop was being bought up by private traders and sold to the Viet Cong. The government placed the collection of rice in the hands of the army but the military was predictably heavy-handed, and in April 1967 some peasants in the district of Samlaut in Battambang province killed two soldiers. The uprising spread to other parts of the country, particularly in the west and in the hill-tribe areas of the north-east. Cambodia's descent into civil war had begun.

Sihanouk could not believe that Cambodian villagers would lift their hands against their king. They were being led astray by leftists with shadowy foreign masters, possibly in China, for many of his most vocal critics in Phnom Penh were Sino-Khmer students. He would treat red Khmer ('Khmers rouges') as he treated those of the right. Bounties were offered, heads were stuck on poles and in cinemas in the capital newsreels of executions by machine gun preceded the main feature, much to the disgust of many in the audience.

With the left out of favour, Sihanouk swung back to the US. In October 1967, Jackie Kennedy came to view the ruins of Angkor. The glamour of the visitor reflected on Sihanouk and paved the way a few months later for a much more substantive visit by Chester Bowles, the American ambassador to India. Sihanouk privately admitted to Bowles what everyone

knew, that Vietnamese communists were using Cambodian territory. He would have no objections, unofficially, if US forces crossed the border in hot pursuit of the enemy. Nixon and Kissinger parleyed hot pursuit into sustained carpet bombing, and over the 14 months from March 1969 there were 3630 B-52 raids inside Cambodia, each bomber capable of obliterating an entire village. The communists, far from being destroyed, retreated deeper into Cambodia, and so the war spread.

Diplomatic relations with Washington were restored in April 1969, but two months later Sihanouk extended recognition to the Provisional Revolutionary Government of the Republic of South Vietnam, which is to say to the Viet Cong. This eased tensions with the communists next door, but not with Washington. In September he compounded the insult by attending the funeral of Ho Chi Minh, the only non-communist Head of State to do so. The Americans were now convinced that the prince was too unstable to be relied upon.

In the late 1960s, journalists would fly in from the slaughterhouse of South Vietnam, relax for the day in Phnom Penh's peaceful, tree-shaded cafes (everyone mentioned the trees), fit in an interview with the ever-available prince and justify their claim for expenses with a glowing report on how well he was governing his country. Or if they did not, if they mentioned, for example, that Buddhist socialism was bankrupt and the villages were slipping out of his grip and that he had lost the support of the cities, they would not be invited back. They could certainly not mention that the military and many civilian leaders looked upon Indonesia's General Suharto, who had recently overthrown the socialist Sukarno, as a hero.

Chief among those who had begun to question Sihanouk's judgement were prime minister

Lon Nol and Prince Sisowath Sirik Matak, the deputy prime minister. Lon Nol had always displayed the utmost devotion to Sihanouk (although there were rumours that he had shot Dap Chhuon in order to prevent news of his own involvement in the Bangkok Plot from becoming known), but it was a devotion built on timidity rather than loyalty. Sirik Matak was by far the stronger personality, and he was infuriated by Sihanouk's toleration of Vietnamese bases inside Cambodia and his failure to come to grips with the economic crisis. Talking to him was impossible: Son Sann, one of his closest and oldest advisors, was shown the door when he tried to explain the state of the country's finances.

ABOVE
A B-52, the iconic American bomber of the Vietnam War.

Sihanouk, cash-strapped and inventive, decided to solve his financial problems by legalizing casinos. He himself regarded gambling as the occupation of fools, but Cambodians from all walks of life, from pedicab drivers to business tycoons, flocked to them. Soon the two casinos, one in Phnom Penh and the other in Sihanoukville, accounted for 9 per cent of budget revenue, but stories of ruin and suicide mounted.

As reality became increasingly unpleasant, Sihanouk retreated into his love of cinema. The first impulse seems traceable to 1964, when Hollywood came to Angkor to make a screen version of Joseph Conrad's classic novel *Lord Jim*, starring Peter O'Toole, fresh from *Lawrence of Arabia*. Filming was cut short by anti-American riots in Phnom Penh, but soon afterwards Sihanouk began turning out a stream of his own films in which he was producer, director, screenwriter and star. At the 1969 Phnom Penh International Film Festival his entry, *Twilight*, won the top award, a solid gold apsara crafted from ingots donated by the national bank.

THE SACRED MOUNTAIN
Cambodia after Sihanouk
Post-1970

OPPOSITE
Cremation of Sihanouk.

Sihanouk was overthrown in March 1970, ushering in the darkest period of Cambodia's modern history. Lon Nol, Sirik Matak and their colleagues acted from genuine concern for Cambodia's future: the economy was stalled, public finances were in tatters and the government had lost control of the eastern provinces. The Head of State had demonstrably failed, and he would not listen to advice. They saw no alternative, and within the framework of Cambodian political life they were right.

FOUNDATIONS OF THE KHMER REPUBLIC

Those who played key roles in Sihanouk's overthrow were, however, wrong in their assumptions about what would happen next. As summed up by David Chandler in *The Tragedy of Cambodian History*, these were, first, that Sihanouk would meekly accept his loss of authority; second, that the Vietnamese would leave Cambodian soil on request, or that the Cambodian army could force them out if they refused; third, that the United States and Cambodia's neighbours would accept Cambodian neutrality, and fourth, that the Cambodian communists would give up their goal of taking over the country.

Washington's involvement continues to be debated. Henry Kissinger denied any US role in Sihanouk's overthrow, but early in 1969 a plan for the assassination of the prince and his replacement by Lon Nol was given blanket approval by the National Security Council. When this was put to Lon Nol he objected that it would spark a popular uprising, and proposed instead a bloodless coup while Sihanouk was out of the country. That, in the end, was what happened, but the course of events suggests improvisation and accident rather than planning.

Sihanouk travelled to France for a regular medical check-up on 4 January 1970. Lon Nol urged him not to stay away too long and started shelling

Vietnamese positions along the border. Sihanouk informed the readers of *Realites Cambodgiennes* that he had had a fine meal of trout with almonds and chicken with Provençal herbs at a charming inn called Chez Dany. In Phnom Penh a mob burnt down the Viet Cong and North Vietnamese embassies, and rioting spread to the provinces. Sihanouk denounced 'personalities aiming... to throw our country into the arms of an imperialist capitalist Power', which he did not identify, and promised to return to sort out the mess shortly. Lon Nol issued an ultimatum to the Viet Cong to leave Cambodia within three days or face the consequences.

On 13 March, Sihanouk left Paris for Moscow after confiding that he intended to have Lon Nol and Sirik Matak executed when he got home. The comment was secretly recorded and sent to Sirik Matak, who took over command of the police and telephoned Sihanouk requesting him to return at once. Sihanouk refused.

BELOW
*Khmer Rouge 'uniform'
– black pyjama-suit, red
checked scarf, rubber
sandals.*

Even now Lon Nol hesitated, and it was only when Sirik Matak came to his house and threatened to shoot him that he signed the paper. On 18 March 1970, the National Assembly endorsed the removal of the Head of State from office pending national elections. The streets were mostly quiet, but schoolchildren celebrated on cue. 'Today we shout, "*A bas le roi*," ' a giggling 15-year-old told a reporter. 'If tomorrow he returns, we shout, "*Vive le roi!*"'

Sihanouk was on his way to Beijing when he received the news. His first reaction was to sound out the French about the possibility of a life in exile, but his old friend Zhou Enlai persuaded him to throw in his lot with the Khmer Rouge. On 23 March he broadcast an appeal to the Cambodian people to take up arms against Lon Nol. Pro-Sihanouk demonstrations broke out in several towns and were put down with brutality, and such was the prince's charisma that tens of thousands of young Cambodians left to join the communists in the jungle, among them the young Hun Sen.

Yet for every Hun Sen there was a young

urban Cambodian who flocked to sign up in Lon Nol's army. Sent against the battle-hardened Vietnamese they were killed in thousands. As if to compensate for battlefield failure, Lon Nol unleashed a pogrom against Vietnamese civilians in Cambodia, the main effect of which was to provoke an anti-Cambodian backlash in South Vietnam. In May, US and South Vietnamese forces invaded the eastern provinces. Lon Nol, realizing that this would only drive the communists deeper into Cambodia, condemned the action as a breach of his country's sovereignty, but he was totally dependent on American military and economic aid, and hostage to events he could not control.

ABOVE
Operation Eagle Pull, 12 April 1975: the Americans leave Phnom Penh.

By the end of 1970, Lon Nol had lost most of the country. Roads and rivers were unsafe, trade had all but ceased and refugees had doubled the population of the capital. Government offensives in 1970 and 1971 (Operations Chenla I and Chenla II) failed miserably and thereafter there were no more. Lon Nol's army commanders turned to amassing wealth, stuffing their battalions with phantom soldiers and pocketing the pay, charging troops for food, uniforms and bullets, and selling their American-donated supplies to the communists.

Cambodia became the Khmer Republic on 9 October 1970, the first time it had been without a king in its history. Sirik Matak began by believing he could control Lon Nol, but instead it was he who was driven from office by Lon Nol and his brother, Lon Non. The latter steadily concentrated power in his hands, appointing and then dismissing the veteran anti-Sihanouk nationalist Son Ngoc Thanh as prime minister, holding rigged elections, closing newspapers and suppressing the opposition. Before long he was ruling as de facto monarch, spending his time begging the Americans for more assistance, erasing enemy units from maps when they could not be removed from the battlefield and searching out magical solutions to his problems.

If Lon Nol put his faith in magic, the Americans put theirs in air power. More than a 100,000 tons of bombs were dropped on Cambodia by 27 January 1973, when the Paris Peace Accords concluded the war between America and Vietnam, and allowed the withdrawal of North Vietnamese troops from the country. This did not mean the end of American air support for Lon Nol, however, and more tonnage was dropped in the next three months than in the entire previous year. The bombing continued until August 1973, when it was ended by the US Congress. In September outgoing US ambassador to Cambodia Emory Swank called this 'Indochina's most useless war', and California Congressman Pete McCloskey later spoke of American destruction of Cambodia as 'a greater evil than we have done to any country in the world'.

In March 1974, the Khmer Rouge took Udong, and by the beginning of 1975 Phnom Penh was cut off from the outside world. The population could not be fed, nor could the army be resupplied except by air. Peace

BELOW
Bomb craters, Kandal province.

LEFT
Pol Pot, May 1978.

proposals were rejected by Sihanouk, who demanded Lon Nol's removal as a precondition to talks. On 1 April 1975, Lon Nol resigned and flew off to exile in America. Alarming rumours were circulating about the Khmer Rouge – how they shot prisoners and herded townspeople into the forest – but as the perimeter tightened and the end neared there were hopes that Khmers could live together in peace.

DEMOCRATIC KAMPUCHEA

The Khmer Rouge entered Phnom Penh on 17 April 1975, and left on 7 January 1979, when they were forced out by Vietnamese forces. They are linked today with the name of Pol Pot, but although he was the leading figure in the regime he was not alone. He had colleagues and he had rivals, even within the party, and his hold on power was never absolutely secure.

Saloth Sar, to give him his original name, was born in 1925 in the village of Prek Sbauv in Kampong Thom province. His father was a well-off farmer who owned 20ha (50 acres) of land, and an aunt was a leading dancer in the Royal Ballet. Those who knew him say he was an adorable child.

The vast majority of children in those years received no education beyond what the local monastery could offer, but his father's comparative wealth and palace connections allowed the young Saloth Sar to complete his primary schooling in Phnom Penh, then enrol at the prestigious Lycée

ABOVE
Khieu Samphan.

Sisowath. There his schoolmates included Khieu Samphan, the future Khmer Rouge Brother Number 4, and Khieu Samphan's two sisters, one of whom was to become his wife. The Khieu siblings were the children of a well-known judge who had run off to Battambang to live with a royal princess, and the other Khieu sister eventually married Ieng Sary, another schoolmate at Lycée Sisowath and the son of a Chinese mother and a wealthy Kampuchea Krom father. The other members of the future Khmer Rouge inner circle came from similar circumstances: Nuon Chea, future Brother Number 2, was the son of a farmer-cum-trader, and studied at Bangkok's Thammasat University while working part-time for the Thai foreign ministry, Ta Mok, Brother Number 5, was from a prosperous landowning family, and Son Sen, later in charge of the Khmer Rouge security apparatus, was the son of a minor landowner in southern Vietnam.

The students of Lycée Sisowath were politically aware, and in 1947 the 19-year-old Saloth Sar worked alongside Ieng Sary in the election campaign

KHMER ROUGE TRIBUNAL

The Extraordinary Chambers in the Courts of Cambodia, popularly the Khmer Rouge Tribunal, commenced work in July 2006.

As of 2018, three former Khmer Rouge leaders, Nuon Chea, Khieu Samphan and Kaing Guek Eav, alias Deuch, had been sentenced to life imprisonment, Ieng Sary had died while awaiting trial, and charges against his wife had been dropped when she developed dementia. It seems unlikely that any more will be tried, and critics question whether this represents an acceptable outcome in terms of justice, let alone value for money ($300 million). They point also to problems of corruption (the Cambodian staff have gone on strike for prolonged periods over unpaid wages), and even more seriously to the persistent and largely successful efforts of the Cambodian government to restrict cases to the top tier of the Khmer Rouge leadership.

Defenders of the Tribunal point to what the trials have meant to many thousands of survivors (more than 236,000 Cambodians have attended the proceedings and many more have followed them in the media), to the substantial impact they have had on public consciousness, and to their role in establishing the rule of law in a society where the concept of accountability remains novel.

It was perhaps inevitable that the Tribunal's work would become politicized, but as several observers have noted, the fact that any trials at all were held is a significant achievement.

of the Democrat Party. Two years later, probably as a reward for his work in the party, the Democrat-controlled Ministry of Education gave him a scholarship to study in Paris.

Almost all the members of the future Khmer Rouge inner circle were in Paris. The city was buzzing with the news and theory of third-world liberation, and inevitably they were drawn further into radical left-wing politics. The most significant document to come out of this time was Khieu Samphan's 1959 doctoral dissertation, 'Cambodia's Economy and Industrial Development'. In it he traced the causes of Cambodia's backwardness to its subordinate place in international capitalism, which sucked away Cambodia's wealth and kept her poor. The cities were outposts of the international capitalist system, and they were not truly Cambodian. Those who lived in them were unproductive, only peasants and the land were productive, and while soldiers and bureaucrats had their uses, 'the greater the reduction in numbers of individuals concerned with general social organization, the greater the number who can contribute to production and the faster the enrichment of the nation'.

In dribs and drabs the young friends returned to Phnom Penh and threw themselves into radical politics. Communism in Sihanouk's Cambodia was a vocation for the dedicated. Party activists faced arrest, torture and there

ABOVE
Ieng Sary.

BELOW
The trial of Nuon Chea.

were disappearances; membership could be counted in the hundreds rather than the thousands. Many, including Saloth Sar, fled to the jungle, and in 1968 they took advantage of the Samlaut uprising to launch an armed uprising.

Still the party had no more than a few hundred activists. The situation changed in 1969 when Richard Nixon ordered the American Air Force to begin Operation Menu. 'Anything that flies on everything that moves,' said Henry Kissinger, and a single B-52 could obliterate an entire village. Operation Menu merged into Operation Freedom Deal, and by 1973 the Americans had dropped the equivalent of five Hiroshimas on eastern Cambodia. Kissinger later swore that there was no link between the bombing and the rise of the Khmer Rouge, but in 2009 Comrade Deuch, the commander of the Tuol Sleng interrogation centre, told the Khmer Rouge war crimes tribunal that 'Mr Richard Nixon and Kissinger allowed the Khmer Rouge to grasp golden opportunities'.

The American bombing was not the whole story. Equally important was the fact that South Vietnamese operations drove the Khmer Rouge into the interior where, shielded by the North Vietnamese and with the charisma of Sihanouk's titular leadership, they could engage in direct recruitment. At the beginning of 1970 there were perhaps 800 KR fighters, by the end of the year there were 12,000, 35,000 in 1972 and 40,000 in 1973, when North Vietnamese troops withdrew. On their own, as they were proud to remember, the communists survived American air power, outfought the Lon Nol forces and took control of Phnom Penh two weeks before the fall of Saigon.

The leadership's first step on taking control of the country was to empty the cities. The order took even some commanders by surprise, but it was in keeping with Khieu Samphan's analysis of Cambodia's situation. The aim was turn Cambodia into an industrialized modern country, and quickly. Machinery could be purchased abroad, but it would have to be paid for. It followed that the next step would be all about exports.

Before 1970, Cambodia had exported rice and rubber, and in theory the possibilities seemed promising, especially for rice. Cambodian farmers produced less than a ton of rice for each hectare, well below regional averages. Regional and district party cadres were therefore instructed to lift production to 3 metric tons per hectare (1.4 tons per acre) within a year. They would do this using the vastly enhanced labour force at their disposal, its productive capacity transformed by scientific management and the abolition of such feudal vestiges as private property and the family.

The cadres set the people to work. In an arrangement reminiscent, although accidentally, of Angkor, they divided them into three classes. Best treated were the *penh sith*, peasants whose purity had been tested by participation in the armed struggle. There are no reliable statistics, but the *penh sith* probably made up no more than 15 per cent of the total. Below them were the *triem*, whose loyalty had yet to be proved but whose peasant background qualified them to be second in line for rice rations. At the bottom were the 'new people', former city-dwellers who, like the ancient slaves, had no rights at all, not even to food. Given the huge influx of refugees into the towns in the previous years of war, many of these were originally from villages, but this made no difference to their classification, for what counted was not class but purity.

'To keep you is no gain, to lose you is no loss,' was the chilling directive. The number of Cambodians who died during the years of Khmer Rouge rule remains unknown, but 1.8 million is a widely accepted estimate. About 40 per cent were executed (there are over 20,000 'killing fields', mass graves for the victims of executions, scattered around the country), another 40 per cent died unnecessarily from starvation and disease, and the remainder perished from miscellaneous causes.

The leadership's targets proved impossible to meet, but failure could not be admitted. The cadres took what steps they could to hide the truth. Harvests could be misreported, but the Ankar (leadership) kept records of exports. The safer way was to make up the shortfalls by sending rice off for export while reducing the rations of the workers. By 1976, food was scarce, and by 1977 and 1978, famine was spreading.

After interrogation at Tuol Sleng, the Khmer Rouge transported detainees to Choeung Ek on the outskirts of the city for execution. The photograph below shows some of the mass graves excavated at this killing field, and the photograph opposite skulls from the graves stored in the memorial stupa in the grounds.

At first the leadership in Phnom Penh, with its plans and programmes, like the French *résidents* with their typewriters and motor cars, knew nothing of the situation in the countryside. When eventually it came to their attention they leapt to the obvious conclusion: traitors within the party were working to sabotage the revolution. Purges began, and Comrade Deuch's interrogation centre began to fill up with cadres of suspect loyalty, many of them high ranking. Torture produced confessions, confessions confirmed the leaderships' paranoia and the search for enemies intensified.

Purity requires theology, and in 1976 the search for internal enemies turned into a debate about the dates 1951 and 1960. The first was the year in which the Indochinese Communist Party (Indochinese in name only – it was heavily Vietnamese) decided to dissolve itself and constitute national parties

for Vietnam, Cambodia and Laos. The statutes and platform of the Khmer People's Revolutionary Party were handed down to it by the Vietnamese, for there was no suggestion that it would be independent:

> *The Vietnamese Party reserves the right to supervise the activities of its brother parties in Cambodia and Laos ... Later, if conditions permit, the three revolutionary Parties ... will unite to form a single Party, the Party of the Vietnam-Khmer-Lao Federation.*

The second date, 1960, commemorated the momentous meeting in an abandoned railway carriage in the grounds of the Phnom Penh Railway station at which Pol Pot, Ieng Sary and others of the now-ruling circle seized control of the Politburo. 1960 meant Cambodian independence and the leadership of Pol Pot, while 1951 demonstrated a pro-Vietnamese line.

The internal squabble led briefly to Pol Pot's resignation, but by the end of the year the 1951 group had lost the debate. The party was purged and the tiny Pol Pot circle was even more firmly in charge, and yet it felt less, not more, secure. In a speech reminiscent of the oath Suryavarman I demanded of the *tamrvac*, Pol Pot called on cadres to be ever alert for treachery: 'Those who defend us ... should have practice in observing. ... [O]bserve everything, but not so those being observed are aware of it.'

Ankar, unable to believe that the internal enemies were acting alone, looked around for what foreign powers were supporting them, and settled on Vietnam, the ancient enemy of the Khmer people. The foreign ministry drafted a paper detailing the loss of Khmer land to Vietnamese 'land swallowers' over the centuries, and Sihanouk, by then under house arrest in the palace, was told that 'we must make war against Vietnam to get back Kampuchea Krom'.

Beijing was happy to support Cambodian enmity towards Vietnam as a counterweight to Soviet influence in Hanoi. By early 1977, large quantities of Chinese military aid were arriving, and in April, Cambodian troops began mounting large-scale cross-border raids into Vietnam, the most serious in September when four Khmer Rouge divisions invaded Vietnam's Tay Ninh province, massacring civilians and razing villages. The raids were supposed to provoke a spontaneous uprising of the Khmer Krom and the reunification of the Khmer land, but all they produced was anger in Hanoi. Hanoi retaliated in December, sending 60,000 troops plus tanks and artillery into Svay Rieng and Kampong Cham before withdrawing. Ankar was now determined to exterminate the Vietnamese nation. Radio Phnom Penh declared that if each Cambodian soldier killed 30 Vietnamese, only two million troops would be needed.

The search for traitors redoubled, especially in the Eastern Zone, which had failed to stop the December incursion. Tens of thousands of Eastern Zone cadres and inhabitants ('Khmer bodies with Vietnamese minds') were rounded up, sparking a revolt by the Zone command. The revolt in turn provoked an even more brutal crackdown, and perhaps as many as 100,000 people were killed.

Hanoi, for its part, had decided that the 'Pol Pot-Ieng Sary clique' had to be removed, and Radio Hanoi announced the formation of the Kampuchean National United Salvation Front, made up of refugees from the Eastern and Northeastern Zones. The Front had little real military significance, but it provided a cover for what happened at the end of the year.

In December 1978, two American journalists, Elizabeth Becker and Richard Dudman, accompanied by Malcolm Caldwell, a Marxist scholar who had praised the Khmer Rouge revolution, visited Democratic Kampuchea at the invitation of Ieng Sary and the party leadership. The high point of their tour was an interview with Pol Pot, who informed them that the Soviet Union and Vietnam intended to conquer Southeast Asia. The West must stand with Kampuchea or else Vietnamese tanks would be rolling into Bangkok and Singapore. The delivery of this message, presumably, was the sole purpose of the invitation, and there is no reason to think that the leadership was not serious. That night gunmen attacked the guesthouse where the visitors were staying and Caldwell was shot dead. Those responsible have never been identified, but the most popular theory is that they belonged to a faction opposed to Pol Pot. Three days later, on 25 December 1978, North Vietnamese and Salvation Front forces crossed the border into Cambodia.

THE PEOPLE'S REPUBLIC OF KAMPUCHEA

Vietnamese troops entered the outskirts of Phnom Penh at 9.30 a.m. on 7 January 1979, and by 11 a.m. the city was in their hands. Pol Pot fled by helicopter to Thailand, where he received a warm if low-key welcome, and by July 1979 he was being guarded by a Thai military unit in a jungle head-quarters just inside the Cambodian border. 'The Thais say they are neutral,' Chinese Vice-Minister for Foreign Affairs Han Nianlong told Sihanouk, who had escaped to Beijing. 'But they are not neutral ... the Thais are with Pol Pot.'

The Chinese were also with Pol Pot. On 17 February, Premier Deng Xiaoping ordered the People's Liberation Army to teach Hanoi a lesson. The incursion into northern Vietnam lasted a month and demonstrated that Chinese tanks were no match for Soviet anti-tank missiles, that the Maoist abolition of ranks led to chaos on the battlefield and that human-wave assaults meant massive casualties. Vietnam was not taught a lesson, but the leadership of the People's Liberation Army was humiliated and Deng strengthened his grip on power in Beijing.

The third country supporting the Khmer Rouge was the United States.

BELOW
Elizabeth Becker, who interviewed Pol Pot shortly before the end of the Khmer Rouge regime and later gave evidence at the war crimes tribunal.

Due to the Khmer Rouge's atrocious human rights reputation, support could not be open, but National Security Advisor Zbigniew Brzezinski encouraged the Chinese and the Thais to support Pol Pot and Democratic Kampuchea. 'We do not like the Khmer Rouge,' Leonard Woodcock, the US Ambassador in Beijing, told Sihanouk, 'but they are the only credible fighting force in the field.'

In the weeks following the fall of Phnom Penh the Khmer Rouge fell back to the Thai border, destroying food stocks and herding civilians with them. Those who could not keep up were left by the sides of the roads to die. 'They were dying everywhere ... dying of hunger,' said Le Thanh Hieu, an officer leading one of the Vietnamese units following close behind. His men used their combat rations to make a thin rice gruel for the starving Khmers.

More than 630,000 people reached Thailand between 1979 and 1981, some taken there by the Khmer Rouge, most simply fleeing the fighting that now wracked western Cambodia. Many were resettled in third countries, mainly the US and France, but by 1987 there were still 265,000 in nine camps strung along the border, more than half of them under the age of 15. The camps were supposed to be sanctuaries, but in fact they served as rear bases for the war. Men were assigned to the fighting, while women and children became porters carrying supplies through the border minefields. Black marketeers and gangsters thrived, and Task Force 80, a Thai military unit assigned to ensure security, joined the bandits to rob, rape and extort.

The largest and most enduring of the camps was Khao-I-Dang, 20km (12 miles) north of Aranyaprathet. The population there reached 160,000 by March 1980, and violence and theft spiralled out of control after it became the main holding centre for migration to third countries. The other eight camps were controlled by the three anti-Phnom Penh resistance organizations, the Khmer Rouge (which underwent several name changes in its search for a better international image), the Sihanoukist Funcinpec (Front Uni National pour un Cambodge Indépendant, Neutre, Pacifique, et Coopératif), and the Khmer People's National Liberation Front (KPNLF), led by 1960s prime minister Son Sann, who had fallen out with Sihanouk and was now both anti-communist and anti-royalist.

The Khmer Rouge ran their five camps as they had run Cambodia, in an atmosphere of fear and repression, and fielded by far the largest, most disciplined, experienced and active fighting force, with about 20,000–30,000 fighters. The KPNLF's two camps were noted for lawlessness, and the Sihanoukists ran the most orderly camp and the most ineffective militia. Shells from Cambodia sometimes fell into the camps, and sometimes there were gun battles between or within them. In June 1982, under pressure from their foreign backers, the three groups agreed to form a coalition government with Sihanouk as president, Son Sann as prime minister and Khieu Samphan as deputy prime minister. Their unity was as fictional as their claim to be the government of Cambodia, but with American, Chinese and ASEAN support, Democratic Kampuchea took Cambodia's seat at the United Nations.

Meanwhile the Vietnamese-backed People's Republic of Kampuchea had been established in Phnom Penh with Heng Samrin and Chea Sim,

BELOW
Prime Minister Hun Sen at the World Economic Forum, 2016.

183

two veteran communists in their forties, as president and vice-president. Vietnamese advisors were placed throughout the government and party, with Le Duc Tho, co-recipient with Henry Kissinger of the 1973 Nobel Peace Prize, as senior advisor. For Hanoi's information, he drew up personality profiles of the new leadership. Heng Samrin was 'a sincere man ... honoured by many cadres' but 'of low education' and with limited political understanding. He failed to develop a factional following and by the end of the 1980s had become a cypher, although his image continued to appear on party billboards throughout the country. Chea Sim had 'a morally good attitude towards the people' but was 'conciliatory, craven, and undecided'. Unlike Heng Samrin, he was destined to play a significant role in future politics.

All senior figures surrounded themselves with relatives and cronies, leading to a marked lack of talent at the top, and against this lacklustre background the young Hun Sen stood out all the more. Born into a peasant family in Kampong Cham in 1951 and educated in a monastery school in Phnom Penh, he joined the Khmer Rouge in 1970 following Sihanouk's call to arms. He ended up in the Eastern Zone, and in June 1977, as purges mounted, he fled to Vietnam, where he drew attention with his success in organizing the anti-Pol Pot military force. Now foreign minister, he showed a quick intelligence and a willingness to appoint his underlings on the basis of ability. The only one of his colleagues who could match him was the new prime minister, Pen Sovan, but Pen Sovan was independent minded and lacked tact. Late in 1981 he was arrested and flown to Hanoi, where he was jailed and put on a diet of rice gruel and boiled eggs. In the reshuffle that followed, Hun Sen became one of three deputy prime ministers and in 1985 prime minister, a position he has held ever since.

The People's Republic slowly began restoring life to Cambodia as millions made their way home to their villages. Almost no infants or old people had survived, and 70 per cent of the population in the countryside were women. Rice was still in short supply, but vegetable gardens, orchards, maize, manioc and the country's vast fishing resources made up the shortfall, and by the end of 1981 the threat of famine was over. The government, true to its socialist ideals, made a half-hearted attempt to set up model collectives, but the showcase villages were chosen on the basis of family ties. The scheme quickly collapsed under the weight of nepotism, and the traditions of Khmer village life reasserted themselves.

By the end of 1981, Phnom Penh's population had increased from effectively zero to perhaps 400,000. People were desperately poor, but crime was low, public safety was good, and youth gangs and prostitution were non-existent. Ragged children picked over piles of rubbish in front of restaurants where high-ranking policemen quaffed Soviet champagne, but the gap between rich and poor was not as great as it was to become in future decades; Michael Vickery, visiting a minister at his home, was struck by the fact that although the house was large the furniture was simple and the minister's wife did the cooking herself over a charcoal pot, as had generations of Khmer housewives.

Two city markets opened, although they operated under tight control in keeping with the government's socialist principles. Only officials and their families were permitted to have stalls in them (street stalls were prohibited), and as they received part of their salary in subsidised rice, tea, sugar, cigarettes, vegetables and the like, they were well placed to exploit their privilege. Indeed, they were forced to, as their cash salaries were far too low to live on. The markets became the hub of a trading network that linked Bangkok to Saigon, with Chinese and Sino-Khmer merchants buying luxuries in the Thai border camps to sell in Phnom Penh to Vietnamese soldiers and functionaries shopping for families and friends back home.

The war continued, although it was confined to the western provinces. In the dry season the Vietnamese would launch clearance operations and the Khmer Rouge would retreat into the jungles and hills, and in the wet season they would return to burn villages and kidnap farmers. In 1984 they burnt down buildings on the edge of Siem Reap, prompting a dry-season offensive that drove them out of the country altogether. After that the war settled into a pattern of ambushes and close-quarter firefights, while in Phnom Penh the streets and markets began to fill with legless ex-soldiers.

The war effort was borne by the Vietnamese, a strain that Soviet assistance only partly made up. Hanoi would have liked to hand over to Phnom Penh and go home, but an appeal for young Cambodian volunteers willing to give up their lives 'for the revolution, for the people, and for supreme glory' failed to meet its objectives. The party turned to conscription, and there were stories of soldiers chasing farm boys through the rice fields and waiting outside schools to press gang students.

Military conscription had its civilian counterpart in K5, a plan to seal off Cambodia from Thailand with 829km (515 miles) of earth walls, spiked ditches, barbed wire entanglements and minefields. The number of men involved on this massive project is unknown, but one authority estimates 380,000 over the period 1985–1987. The organization of such a workforce – food, clothing, work tools, medical care – would have tested the most competent of administrations, which the People's Republic was not. Workers faced overwork, inadequate food, shelter and medical facilities, malaria, landmines, snakes, accidents and isolation. 'It was like the Khmer Rouge,' one participant remarked years later. But the barrier was built and the two sides settled into a stalemate, with the Vietnamese unable to eliminate the bases over the Thai border, and the Khmer Rouge unable to breach K5.

With the military situation deadlocked, attention turned to diplomacy. Since 1982, Sihanouk had been promoting the idea of a negotiated settlement under international auspices, but Phnom Penh held that there was no international problem to resolve, only an internal one between Khmers. The breakthrough came in 1985 with the elevation of Mikhail Gorbachev to the presidency of the Soviet Union. Like Deng in China, he was a pragmatist and a nationalist, and under his leadership Moscow changed its priority from the defence of international socialism to the salvation of the Soviet economy. Military and economic aid to Hanoi was reduced, and the Vietnamese were advised that they should look at the benefits of *perestroika*, which literally means restructuring but in fact meant capitalism.

Hanoi passed this pressure on to Phnom Penh, and the PRK announced that it was entering on a reform agenda. Private property rights over land and housing were reintroduced, creating a Phnom Penh property boom that continues to the present day, and restrictions on the operation of the market eased. Restrictions on religion were also lifted, and state officials began to patronise the monkhood and traditional celebrations such as the Water Festival. Patronage of religion vastly enhanced the popularity of the prime minister, Hun Sen.

In September 1989, the last Vietnamese forces withdrew from Cambodia and the People's Republic of Kampuchea signalled a new beginning by becoming the State of Cambodia. Buddhism was declared the state religion and socialism was renounced. At the same time, Moscow, Beijing and Washington, brought together by the ending of the Cold War, agreed that they wished to see a neutral, non-communist, non-aligned government led by Sihanouk in Cambodia. Negotiations between the parties intensified, and on 23 October 1991, today a public holiday, the Paris Peace Accords were signed. All foreign military assistance would cease, the parties would disarm, all refugees would be repatriated and a special UN mission, the United Nations Transitional Authority in Cambodia (UNTAC), would organize elections for a Constituent Assembly.

With the signing of the Accords a Supreme National Council came into existence, made up of the State of Cambodia and the three members of the Coalition Government of Democratic Kampuchea. The SNC would take Cambodia's seat at the UN until the new Constitution came into effect, during which period it would share the administration of the country with UNTAC.

ABOVE

Stamps issued in Phnom Penh to commemorate the 5th anniversary of liberation from the Khmer Rouge.

CAMBODIA'S DEMOCRATIC EXPERIMENT

With peace officially restored, the leaders began to gather in Phnom Penh. Sihanouk landed at Pochentong Airport on 14 November 1991, and rode into the city in a 1963 Chevy with Hun Sen beside him. The streets were lined with cheering crowds throwing flowers and calling out his name, but it was clear to observers that while Sihanouk expected to parlay his popularity and diplomatic connections into real power, Hun Sen had no intention of allowing any such thing.

On 27 November, Khieu Samphan, titular head of the Khmer Rouge, landed at Pochentong. Like Sihanouk, he drove to the city along streets lined with crowds, but the crowds were shouting out the names of murdered relatives. He was delivered to a villa surrounded by an angry mob, and within hours he was brought back to the airport in an armoured car with his bleeding head bandaged in a pair of Y-fronts. As he prepared to fly out he was observed in heated discussion with Hun Sen. When tempers cooled, the Khmer Rouge issued a statement saying that they would continue to abide by the peace process, but the omens were not good.

Everyone was looking forward to the arrival of UNTAC's 16,000 troops and 3,600 civilian police, but the peacekeepers were slow in coming. While they delayed, public order was collapsing. Former state employees were protesting against the privatization of their jobs, tenants of state-owned public housing and squatters from the slums were protesting against forced evictions and the sale of their homes, and students were protesting against corruption. The government imposed curfews and arrested demonstrators, and one critic was assassinated.

UNTAC finally arrived in Phnom Penh in March 1992. The first important task, due to begin on 13 June, was to be the supervised disarmament of 70 per cent of each faction's armed forces, but during the months of waiting the Khmer Rouge had attempted to seize as much territory and as many voters as possible, leading to violent clashes with the Cambodian People's Party (CPP). Now the KR announced that they would not disarm, citing the presence of Vietnamese forces and the unfair advantage given the CPP by its continuing control of the state apparatus. The first claim was unfounded, but the latter was not without merit. The KR refused to allow UNTAC's military observers access to its territory, and there was well-publicized footage of the chief of the military mission being turned away from a KR checkpoint by a teenage Khmer Rouge. UNTAC rapidly lost the respect of the public and the parties. 'If there is a fight somewhere,' complained Sihanouk, 'UNTAC does not intervene. On the contrary, it withdraws.'

Having failed to disarm anyone, UNTAC redefined its military mission as the provision of security. For the purposes of the election, Cambodia was divided into 21 constituencies, these being the existing 21 provinces and municipalities. Representation was proportional, meaning that each constituency had multiple seats allocated according to the proportion of votes cast for each party. Organizing, supervising and monitoring the election were some 2,000 UNTAC civilian staff and 50,000 Cambodian staff, with the military and police component of UNTAC providing security. In a difficult but successful operation, 360,000 refugees were repatriated from Thailand and enrolled in their constituencies.

The KR had already announced that it would boycott the election, but 20 political parties registered, the vast majority of them the personal vehicles of prominent or once-prominent politicians who had spent long periods overseas. The only groupings with a claim to a country-wide presence were the CPP, Funcinpec and the Buddhist Liberal Democratic Party, the vehicle of Son San's KPNLF. UNTAC began a programme of voter education, but the CPP obstructed the other parties' access to radio,

BELOW
Flag used by UNTAC – the only Cambodian flag since colonial times not to show Angkor Wat.

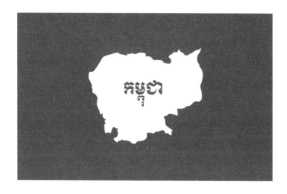

television and printing facilities, all under state control, prompting UNTAC to set up its own radio station. Funcinpec, led by Sihanouk's son, Prince Norodom Ranariddh, capitalized on the ex-king's immense popularity by plastering the country with posters bearing Sihanouk's photo, and when told that that this could not be allowed, with posters of himself bearing a striking resemblance to his father.

The campaign focused on who was best able to restore peace and security. Hun Sen promoted the CPP as the only party with the means to resist the Khmer Rouge, Ranariddh warned that a CPP victory would mean the renewal of war with the Khmer Rouge, and the BLDP and the multitude of personal parties stressed the need to protect Cambodia against the CPP's Vietnamese lackeys. The Khmer Rouge attacked a Vietnamese fishing village near Siem Reap on the Tonle Sap, leading to a mass exodus of Vietnamese and raising fears of further violence.

ABOVE

Office of the Cambodian People's Party, Siem Reap, 2013. The billboard shows the three party leaders Heng Samrin, Hun Sen and Chea Sim, and the statue in the building forecourt is the Party logo, an apsara (heavenly nymph) scattering blessings.

The election took place over 23–28 May 1993. More than four million voters, almost 90 per cent of those eligible, participated. Funcinpec won 58 of the 120 seats with 45.5 per cent of the vote and the CPP won 51 seats and 38.2 per cent of the vote, the remaining seats going to the Buddhist Liberal Democrats (10 seats) and a Funcinpec splinter party (one seat). In Battambang and Kampong Cham, the latter Hun Sen's own constituency, the CPP won only 31 per cent of votes, while in Phnom Penh and Kandal province (the province surrounding the capital), where intimidation and patronage were least effective, it received only 28 per cent against Funcinpec's 58 per cent.

UN Special Representative Yasushi Akashi described the election as 'a stinging rebuke to the men of violence', but Hun Sen felt the result as a personal humiliation. The CPP lodged complaints, claiming voting irregularities, and demanded that voting be rerun in four provinces. There were rumours that Hun Sen was preparing for an armed takeover, and troops surrounded the royal palace. On 3 June, following talks with CPP Chairman Chea Sim and with Ranariddh's reluctant consent, Sihanouk announced that Funcinpec and the CPP would form an interim government in which they would share power equally, with himself acting as arbiter.

The United States had made no secret of its willingness to overturn the deal. 'We can do without Prince Sihanouk,' a senior US official said privately. 'We can do without the CPP. We have ninety million dollars to keep the officials and soldiers of the SOC (State of Cambodia) and to buy the CPP deputies necessary to get the two-thirds (majority needed to form a government) and then put in place the coalition of our choice.' At 5.30 p.m. on 3 June, the embassy issued a statement labelling the interim government a violation of the Accords. Australia, China and the United Kingdom backed the Americans, and Rannariddh joined them. Sihanouk withdrew the proposal. On 10 June, Hun Sen informed Akashi that Prince Norodom Chakrapong, a half-brother of Ranariddh who had joined the SOC, was about to seize control of the eastern provinces and form a secessionist state. 'I can no longer control the situation,' he told UNTAC. Anti-UN demonstrations broke out in several provinces, and ferry operators began refusing services to UN vehicles. Washington, or rather the US embassy, faced with the imminent collapse of the Accords and a return to civil war, withdrew its opposition to the power-sharing agreement. On 14 June, the Constitutional Assembly met in an emergency session and elected Sihanouk as Head of State, and Sihanouk appointed Ranariddh and Hun Sen co-chairmen of the interim government.

UNTAC cost two billion dollars. Cynics would say that the intention had been no more than to disengage the great powers from a dispute that no longer suited a changed international landscape, but for idealists it was a

RIGHT
Ranariddh announces his return to politics, 2015.

test of the international community's commitment to a new post-Cold War world in which democracy was the right of all. Its immediate achievements were large and real: hundreds of thousands of refugees had been brought home and resettled, genuinely free and fair elections had been held in conditions of security, and the basic institutions of a liberal democracy had been put in place. On the other side of the ledger, the CPP showed every sign of intending to remain in power no matter what future elections might decide, the Khmer Rouge remained in play, and Cambodia was impoverished and littered with landmines. The next few decades would reveal whether the pessimists or the optimists were right.

GETTING TO 1997

Cambodia's post-UNTAC Constitution came into effect on 24 September 1993, when the Constitutional Assembly was transformed into a National Assembly. In keeping with their power-sharing agreement, Prince Ranariddh became First Prime Minister and Hun Sen Second Prime Minister, and each party took control of 11 ministries, with two key ministries of Interior and Defence under joint control. Funcinpec's former fighters were merged into the national army and national police, which were also under joint command.

Cooperation was harmonious at first, especially when it concerned joint survival. In July the two prime ministers combined to put down a coup attempt led by Prince Chakrapong (although Chakrapong denied involvement), and later acted swiftly to sack Sam Rainsy, the Funcinpec-appointed finance and development minister, when he launched an anti-corruption campaign that offended business interests. But in general Ranariddh was passive. His passivity allowed the CPP to strengthen its grip on public administration, and soon Funcinpec's inability to deliver benefits to its constituents (while the CPP could), and a growing reputation for corruption, were eroding the party's standing with the public and Ranariddh's standing in the party.

Sam Rainsy, who was the son of the Sam Sary who had opposed Sihanouk at the time of the Bangkok Plot, rapidly emerged as a significant political figure. He spent 1995 building a profile as a campaigner against corruption, and when he announced that he was forming his own party Funcinpec suffered a wave of defections. Ranariddh, galvanized at last, made a speech in March 1996 complaining about the CPP's failure to share district chief positions with Funcinpec (meaning his own failure to procure rewards for his supporters) and threatened to withdraw from the coalition.

Meanwhile the Khmer Rouge were disintegrating. In August 1996, Ieng Sary, now ruling a KR enclave at Pailin, defected to Phnom Penh, bringing a quarter of the Khmer Rouge troops with him. Financed by his continuing control of Pailin's gem mines, he retired to a luxury villa in the capital while his 3,000 troops joined the national army. Ranariddh now put out feelers to the remaining Khmer Rouge leaders, who controlled 2,000 troops at their headquarters at Anlong Veng in the north-west. Hun Sen accused Ranariddh of hiding KR fighters in the Funcinpec base at Tang Kraisang near Pochentong Airport, and relations were not eased by a violent clash between CPP and Funcinpec troops in Battambang.

The new year opened in a state of high tension as the 1998 elections approached. Ranariddh and Sam Rainsy formed a National United Front, and Hun Sen engineered a split in Funcinpec that cost the party its majority in the Assembly. In March a grenade attack on a Rainsy rally killed 19 people and wounded up to 150, and a subsequent investigation by the FBI (called in because an American citizen was among the victims) implicated Hun Sen's personal bodyguard unit. Leaders of all parties began strengthening their personal bodyguards – every public figure of note had such units, Ranariddh's numbering 1,000 men, Hun Sen's 1,500. On 26 May, authorities in Sihanoukville announced the seizure of two tons of weapons and

RIGHT
Mine museum, Siem Reap. In the first six months of 2017 six people were killed by mines and other explosions, and ten had limbs amputated.

ammunition in crates addressed to Ranariddh. Two days later someone fired a shot at Hun Sen (his brother-in-law had been assassinated the previous November), and the Second Prime Minister accused the First Prime Minister of preparing for a coup.

On 2 June, Nhek Bun Chhay, the Funcinpec Minister of Defence, announced that Khieu Samphan would rejoin mainstream politics and bring the remaining KR troops with him. On 5 June, Hun Sen made a speech reminding Khieu Samphan of what happened the last time he returned to Phnom Penh.

On 10 June, Pol Pot ordered the execution of Son Sen and his family (they were shot and their bodies were run over by a truck), and was carried off into the jungle on a litter, intravenous drip lines dangling from his arms. With him he took Ranariddh's dialogue partner Khieu Samphan. 'I would like to inform you that the Khmer Rouge problems in Anlong Veng are reaching a level of complexity that we cannot understand,' Ranariddh told journalists.

On 14 June, government soldiers near Anlong Veng reported gunfire from the direction of Khmer Rouge territory, and on 17 June Anlong Veng radio denounced Pol Pot for acts of treason carried out in the previous week. The situation was now resolved, the announcement said, and the Khmer Rouge under Khieu Samphan's leadership would support the National United Front (that is, Ranariddh) in the struggle against Vietnam and its lackies (that is, Hun Sen). That evening a gunfight broke out on Monivong Boulevard between the bodyguards of Ranariddh and those of Hok Lundy, the CPP police chief.

On 21 June, the two prime ministers appeared together in public to announce that Pol Pot had been arrested in Anlong Veng and would be brought before an international tribunal to face trial. The show of unity did not last beyond the press conference. In the last week of June CPP, troops began confronting and disarming their Funcinpec counterparts, and on 4 July news reached Hun Sen that an agreement had been hammered out between Ranariddh and Khieu Samphan. That evening Ranariddh, warned

ABOVE
The royal arms. At the centre the Preah Khan, or state sword, rests on an urn; above it is the state crown, radiating light; lions at either side support royal parasols.

BELOW
Sam Rainsy.

that he was about to be arrested or killed, boarded a flight for Paris.

By dawn the next morning, forces loyal to Hun Sen had closed the airport and surrounded Funcinpec strong points, including Ranariddh's home. Funcinpec tanks and infantry broke through the cordon surrounding their military base at Tang Krasaing near the airport and moved down Russian Boulevard towards the city, aiming to link up with their comrades inside Ranariddh's compound. Their commander halted the advance when he reached the Royal University of Phnom Penh, unwilling to become responsible for the loss of civilian lives that would follow if he entered the city centre. It was the humane decision, but it doomed Funcinpec to defeat.

For the next three days the spoils went to the victors. The airport was looted down to the toilet fittings, shops and warehouses were stripped, and citizens looked on helplessly as soldiers and police entered their homes and took what they wanted, from television sets to pots and pans and bundles of clothes. (Not all the vandalism was being done by the military: a bar patronized by Westerners was trashed by neighbours getting their revenge for too many nights of ear-splitting music.) Then the rubble was cleared from the streets, cafes and schools reopened, and businesses began restocking, but for weeks the bodies of executed Funcinpec officials turned up on the outskirts of the city with tongues ripped out and penises stuffed in their mouths.

TIGER ON THE MOUNTAIN

The CPP called 5 July a 'special event', but the outside world called it a coup. Aid was frozen, Cambodia's candidacy for ASEAN was put on hold and its membership of the UN was effectively suspended. Hun Sen became conciliatory. The elections would go ahead as scheduled, Funcinpec was free to contest them, and even Ranariddh was welcome to return, although he must face trial.

Grudgingly, the foreign community accepted Hun Sen's reality. It had too much invested in the success of the UNTAC experiment. In any case, many were glad to be rid of Ranariddh, who had played the same game as Hun Sen and played it badly. 'There are no heroes in Cambodia,' commented a senior Clinton White House official. 'Nobody's black or white; they're all shades of gray.' An understanding was reached whereby Ranariddh was tried, fined $54 million for the damage and granted a royal pardon.

The 1998 elections went ahead as scheduled. Journalists pointed out that the lead-up was characterized by intimidation and coercion, and that voting had taken place under the eyes of Hok Lundy's police. However, the two main international observer groups, mindful of the need to bring Cambodia back into the community of nations, declared it a credible reflection of the popular will. Funcinpec and the newly formed Sam Rainsy Party won more votes than the CPP, but as a result of a last-minute revision of the electoral rules the CPP ended up with a slim majority in the National Assembly.

The opposition refused to accept the outcome. Funcinpec and the Sam Rainsy Party joined hands and swore they would deny the CPP the 60 per cent majority needed to form a government unless their joint demands were met. Ranariddh and Sam Rainsy stood shoulder to shoulder through three months of haggling and street demonstrations, until the CPP offered Funcinpec a deal whereby Hun Sen became sole prime minister, Ranariddh was given the presidency of the Senate, and Rainsy was left at the altar.

The next round was Cambodia's first-ever commune-level elections in 2002 (in the Cambodian administrative structure several villages make up a commune, communes make up districts and districts make up provinces). The Western community had high hopes that these would see a blossoming of grassroots democracy, but the CPP party structure was intertwined with the civil administrative structure, with all that meant in terms of patronage and manipulation, and the CPP won 1,597 of the 1,621 positions. The EU Election Observation Mission testified that the vote was free and fair, but a coalition of NGOs issued a joint statement citing numerous irregularities, ranging from intimidation to murder.

Cambodia's third post-UNTAC general elections were held in 2003. Once more the CPP fell short of the two-thirds majority needed to form a government, and Ranariddh and Sam Rainsy renewed their solidarity pact, offering a coalition to the CPP in return for Hun Sen's resignation. As before, there was haggling and demonstrations, and as before Ranariddh dropped Rainsy in return for plum positions in government for himself and his colleagues.

Rainsy's revenge on Ranariddh came in 2006, when he backed a Constitutional amendment allowing a government to form with a simple 50 per cent majority in the National Assembly. As Hun Sen no longer needed Ranariddh, the coalition was dissolved and Funcinpec ministers were given the choice between losing their jobs or joining Hun Sen. Many chose Hun Sen, and others retired from public life.

Ranariddh's place at the forefront of the opposition movement was taken by Sam Rainsy and prominent human rights activist Kem Sokha, both with reputations for personal integrity. In 2013 their Khmer National Rescue Party won 55 seats to 68 for the CPP, and at the commune elections in mid-2017 they won 40 per cent of the local councils despite all the hurdles placed in their way by an unequal system. It seemed that the party might have a real chance of winning the 2018 Assembly elections, but by the end of the year Rainsy had fled into self-imposed exile, Sokha was in jail facing charges of conspiring with the United States to overthrow the government and the Khmer National Rescue Party had been dissolved by the courts. Ranariddh, now in his seventies, supported the move, expecting the CNRP's seats to be allocated to Funcinpec. 'Samdech Hun Sen, you want or you don't want, you like him or you don't like him, he brings about this national unity,' the prince explained.

Meanwhile, less visibly but no less significantly, Hun Sen was strengthening his dominance over the CPP. As recently as 1990, the *Los Angeles Times* had identified party president Chea Sim as the strongman of Cambodia, as although Hun Sen was prime minister with an impressive patronage base, Chea Sim controlled what old-school Marxists would have recognized as the real sources of power, the police and the party security apparatus. Anyone wishing to bet on who would be in control of Cambodia a decade hence might have put their money on the head of the party rather than the head of government.

Chakrapong's brief revolt in 1994 was a serious affair involving 200–300 soldiers in a dozen armoured personnel carriers. He was joined by General Sin Song, a key supporter of Chea Sim, and it was lack of confidence in Chea Sim and the regular army that led Hun Sen to use Funcinpec troops to put the revolt down. It was an important lesson for Hun Sen, who in the aftermath placed the police under the command of Hok Lundy, one of his key factional commanders, and set about building up a military force loyal to himself alone. When Hun Sen cracked down on Ranariddh and Funcinpec in 1997, he used his own bodyguard and loyalist Khmer Rouge forces, and the Chea Sim faction remained on the sidelines. As gunfire crackled around the city they barricaded their homes, fearing that they might be the next targets. They survived, but in the following years the key positions in government, the military and the party were filled by Hun Sen, and Chea Sim became increasingly irrelevant, though he was still capable of a last flicker of defiance. This came in 2004 when, as acting Head of State, he refused to sign off on the CPP/Funcinpec power-sharing arrangement because the Senate, created in 1999 as a sinecure for himself and his faction, was to be given to Ranariddh. According to several sources the situation almost came to violence, but it ended with Chea Sim being bundled onto a flight to Bangkok by Hok Lundy's police while a Hun Sen loyalist signed the necessary papers. That loyalist, ironically, was Nhek Bun Chhay, one-time *consigliere* to Ranariddh, but by now a high-ranking CPP apparatchik.

Today, Hun Sen controls all formal levers of state and party, as well as the media, business, the security apparatus (police, armed forces and intelligence services) and the judiciary, but as power has consolidated in his hands the formal mechanisms have grown increasingly irrelevant and he rules through family and patronage, unchallenged and unchallengeable, and increasingly impatient with opposition.

THE NEW MILLENNIUM

In October 2004, Sihanouk announced his intention to abdicate:

> *I have had the great honour to serve the nation and people for more than half a century. I am getting old, my body and my pulse are getting weaker. It is up to the Royal Throne Council to decide whether Prince Sihamoni or who else will be an appropriate successor to Norodom Sihanouk.*

AIDING DEMOCRACY

In *Aid Dependence in Cambodia: How Foreign Assistance Undermines Democracy*, Sophal Ear traces the relationship between foreign aid and Cambodia's failure to develop democratic institutions: 'Foreign aid has crippled the government's political will to tax, and without taxation the link between government accountability and popular elections is broken.' His prescription for fixing the broken system is to wean Cambodia off foreign aid (including NGOs) and strengthen tax collection, thus re-establishing the link between representation and taxation. However, with China now replacing Western donors as the main source of aid and investment, the odds are that Cambodia's government will continue to be disconnected from any need to tax its citizens.

Ranariddh made no secret of his conviction that he should be that successor, but Sihanouk believed that his eldest son's autocratic style and lack of tact would inevitably lead to conflict and perhaps imperil the very existence of the monarchy. Sihamoni was the most suitable candidate precisely because he had no desire to be king. Born in 1953, he had grown up in Europe and graduated from the Academy of Performing Arts in Prague. In obedience to his father's wish, he returned with him to Phnom Penh during the Khmer Rouge period and endured house arrest in the palace. Afterwards, as Cambodia's delegate to UNESCO in Paris, he displayed a capacity for hard work and a devotion to Cambodian culture. Reigning as a constitutional symbol of Khmer identity, he has proven an ideal monarch for Cambodia in the modern age.

Modern Cambodia could not have been imagined in 1997. In 2015, the World Bank reclassified it from low-income to lower middle-income status, capping two decades of growth averaging 7.5 per cent each year. In that time poverty has more than halved, and key social indicators, including life expectancy, maternal health and access to primary education, have all shown marked improvement. New employment opportunities in tourism and the garment and construction industries have sparked massive urban migration as young people seek to escape the poverty of the villages, and today around 20 per cent of the population lives in towns and cities. Cambodians today are more prosperous than at any time in their history, and Hun Sen's government deserves credit for the achievement.

Booming growth has come at significant cost to the natural environment. An explosion of dam building on the Mekong River has led to grave fears about the future of Cambodia's fisheries and rice lands, forest cover is now below 50 per cent and is still falling rapidly, and the wildlife trade, fed by apparently insatiable demand from China, has led to the extinction of practically all large mammals in the wild. Mangrove forests are threatened by coastal development, the construction industry's demand for sand and limestone is destroying beaches and riverbanks, and archaeological sites throughout the country are in danger of being destroyed before they are even discovered. The government is aware of the dangers and steps are being taken to meet them, but whether these will be sufficient, or enforced with sufficient vigour, remains in question.

Hun Sen is seen by many in the West as a dictator, but he views himself, not without cause, as the architect of today's peace and prosperity. He warns the people that this present condition is recent and fragile, and asks them to look back to the peasant-king Sdech Kan, who came from humble beginnings to lead Cambodia to greatness before chaos once again engulfed the land. But half of all Cambodians today are below 25 years of age, and the chaos of the Khmer Rouge period, or even of the turbulent years leading up to 1997, are not part of their memory. Warnings of chaos mean little to them. They are better educated and more in touch with the world than their parents, and the past has correspondingly little sway over them. The challenge facing Cambodia today is to manage their expectations for tomorrow.

LEFT
Cambodia has made significant progress in promoting education. However, challenges remain with access, quality and gaps in the implementation of many policies.

OVERLEAF
Contemporary Phnom Penh.

TIMELINE

PREHISTORY TO FIRST KINGDOMS

Prehistory The first Cambodians are nomadic hunter-gatherers, probably ethnically Australo-Melanesian. Austroasiatic-speaking immigrants from southern China introduce rice after c. 2200 BC. Settled villages and tribal societies appear. Metal technology is introduced after c. 1000 BC. Population density increases, trade networks expand to South Asia and China, tribes become chiefdoms and proto-states form.

4th century BC–2nd century AD Site of Angkor Borei occupied. Oc Eo culture emerges around the 1st century BC–1st century AD, with major urban centres at Angkor Borei and Oc Eo, the latter apparently an entrepot (half-way house) on the trade route between South Asia and China.

3rd–5th centuries First mention of the name Funan in Chinese records, early 3rd century, although the name never appears in local inscriptions and has no known meaning. First tribute missions to the Chinese court. Increasing adoption of Indic culture. Early rulers bear indigenous names prefixed with a title that might be *pon*; later kings have Sanskrit names ending in *varman*.

6th century Decline of Funan as trade routes shift away from the delta. Emergence of Khmer-speaking inland states based on control of rice and population through the mechanism of the temple. Bhavavarman I and successors create a decentralized inland polity conventionally called Chenla.

7th–8th centuries Jayavarman I expands and centralizes the kingdom (mid–late 7th century). Little is known about the century following his death, but it was apparently a time of multiple political centres.

ANGKOR

Early period 9th–10th centuries Jayavarman II unifies the various states c. 770–800 and establishes his capital in the Angkor plain. The new kingdom shows strong continuity with the preceding Chenla period, including Indic culture and a political system based on family and temples. Under subsequent kings a sense of national identity develops.

Middle period 11th–12th centuries Angkor becomes become increasingly sophisticated and centralized. Expansion into modern Thailand and central Vietnam (ancient Champa) under Suyrvarman I, Suryavarman II and Jayavarman VII.

Late period 13th–early 15th centuries Angkor loses control over outlying areas. Theravada Buddhism becomes increasingly popular and is adopted as the royal cult. In the second half of the 14th century, climate change stresses the Angkorian irrigation system, and in the first half of the 15th century Angkor is occupied by Siam.

EARLY MODERN PERIOD

15th–mid-17th centuries Kings move their capital to the Phnom Penh/Longvek/Udong area, probably to take advantage of the increasing tempo of maritime trade. The economic base of the kingdom changes from control of rice to control of commerce. Cambodia remains an important regional power, the equal of Siam and Nguyen (central) Vietnam.

Late 17th–early 19th centuries Rivalry within the royal clan leads to repeated intervention by Siam and Nguyen Vietnam, ending in a major civil war in the early 19th century from which the pro-Siamese faction emerges victorious (1847). Vietnam is in rapid decline under French pressure. King Ang Duong makes overtures to France but the French response is maladroit.

FRENCH PROTECTORATE AND INDEPENDENCE

Early French Protectorate (1860–1904) King Norodom signs a treaty of protection with France. The French Protectorate becomes increasingly intrusive until Cambodian sovereignty is effectively lost.

The *Roitelets* (1904–1940) Cambodia's kings are figureheads but the prestige of kingship rises. The

French restore the western provinces and give Cambodia secure borders with Thailand. They modernize administration but fail to educate Cambodians. First stirrings of nationalism.

Second World War (1940–1945) French prestige is undermined by military humiliation. Japanese-sponsored 'independence' is overturned by France at the end of the war, but US insistence on decolonization means that the Protectorate must end.

Independence (1945–1970) King Sihanouk achieves full independence. Cambodia is bequeathed a democratic constitution modelled on the French Fourth Republic, but it quickly descends into squabbling and paralysis. Sihanouk reverts to autocracy. After several years of prosperity the Vietnam War and economic mismanagement provoke a coup.

CONTEMPORARY PERIOD

Civil war and the Khmer Rouge (1975–1978) Civil war and the victory of the Khmer Rouge. Their attempt to modernize Cambodia through scientific socialism results in massive suffering.

Civil war resumed (1979–1991) The Khmer Rouge provoke a Vietnamese invasion. Civil war resumes, now between the Vietnamese-backed government in Phnom Penh and Khmer Rouge and royalist forces in Thailand with Thai, Western and Chinese patronage. UN-sponsored Paris peace agreement signed in 1991.

UNTAC (1992–1993) The international community leaves Cambodia with a democratic constitution, but its operation is compromised by the persistence of traditional patronage-based norms among political leaders.

After UNTAC (1993–present) Hun Sen, Prime Minister, consolidates control. After 1997, political stability and rapid economic growth bring peace and highly unequal prosperity, but environmental challenges, demographic forces and the lack of outlets for democratic aspirations raise questions about the future.

PUBLICATIONS

Becker, Elizabeth, *When the War was Over: Cambodia and the Khmer Rouge Revolution* (Public Affairs, 1998).

Bizot, Francois, *The Gate* (Harvill Press, 2003).

Boswell, Steven, *King Norodom's Head* (NIAS Press, 2016).

Chandler, David, *A History of Cambodia* (Avalon Publishing, 2009).

Edwards, Penny, *Cambodge: The Cultivation of a Nation, 1860–1945* (University of Hawaii Press, 2007).

Harris, Ian, *Cambodian Buddhism: History and Practice* (Silkworm Books, 2005).

Jacobsen, Trudy, *Lost Goddesses: The Denial of Female Power in Cambodian History* (NIAS Press, 2008).

Kiernan, Ben, *The Pol Pot Regime: Race, Power, and Genocide in Cambodia Under the Khmer Rouge, 1975–79* (Yale University Press, 2014).

Mizerski, Jim, *Cambodia Captured: Angkor's First Photographers in 1860s Colonial Intrigues* (Jasmine Image Machine, 2016).

Mouhot, Henri, *Travels in the Central Parts of Indo-China (Siam), Cambodia, and Laos, During the Years 1858, 1859 and 1860* (Cambridge University Press, 2016).

Muller, Gregor, *Colonial Cambodia's 'Bad Frenchmen'* (Routledge, 2006).

O'Reilly, Dougald, *Early Civilizations of Southeast Asia* (Rowman Altamira, 2007).

Osborne, Milton, *Sihanouk: Prince of Light, Prince of Darkness* (Allen & Unwin, 1994).

Osborne, Milton, *Phnom Penh: A Cultural and Literary History* (Signal Books, 2008).

Osborne, Milton, *Southeast Asia: An Introductory History*, 12th edn (Allen & Unwin, 2016).

Reid, Anthony, *A History of Southeast Asia* (Wiley Blackwell, 2015).

Rooney, Dawn, *Angkor* (Odyssey, 2011).

Shawcross, William, *Sideshow: Nixon, Kissinger, and the Destruction of Cambodia* (New York, 1979).

Short, Philip, *Pol Pot: Anatomy of a Nightmare* (Henry Holt and Company, 2007).

Strangio, Sebastian, *Hun Sen's Cambodia* (Silkworm Books/Yale University Press, 2014).

Van der Kran, Alfons, *Murder and Mayhem in 17th Century Cambodia* (Brill Academic, 2009).

Zhou Daguan (trans. Peter Harris), *A Record of Cambodia* (Silkworm Book, 2007).

INDEX

Page numbers denoting illustrations are highlighted in **bold**.

PICTURE CREDITS